FROM PHONOLOGY TO PHILOLOGY:

An Outline of Descriptive and Historical Spanish Linguistics

John R. Burt

University Press of America

Library of Congress Cataloging in Publication Data

Burt, John R
From phonology to philology.

Bibliography: p.
Includes index.
1. Spanish language. I. Title.
PC4071.B8   460   80-67212
ISBN 0-8191-1310-7
ISBN 0-8191-1311-5 (pbk.)

460
B973f

For Joyce and Angela

Acknowledgements:

I wish to take this opportunity to thank my former professor at the University of Minnesota, Professor Ricardo A. Narváez, without whom this book would have never been written. His patience, wisdom and sincerity have been imparted freely to those of us fortunate enough to have known him.

I wish also to thank my wife Joyce for her support and for her unwavering faith.

TABLE OF CONTENTS

INTRODUCTION

Definition of LINGUISTICS

The purpose of this book is to serve as an introduction to Spanish linguistics for those who have had little or no previous background in linguistics. In large part the book is an introduction to linguistic terminology, and in keeping with this aim, all the major terms will be given in English and in Spanish, and will be defined at the time of their introduction in the text and also in the Bilingual Glossary (pp. 165-88).

LINGUISTICS (Lingüística) we define as the scientific study of language, and our study of Spanish linguistics will therefore constitute a scientific examination of the Spanish language. We shall examine the descriptive phonology and morphology of modern Spanish as well as its historical sound changes and semantic and lexical development from Latin.

Definition of LANGUAGE

To begin our study of the Spanish language we need first to approach a definition of LANGUAGE (idioma). While many acceptable definitions already exist, we prefer to define it through description: a language consists of a system of sounds (phonology) which conveys meaning (morphology, semantics) when delivered orally or in writing within the accepatble limits of its structure (syntax, grammar).

All the known languages of the world have or have had a system of sounds, even those which are no longer spoken and which are known to us only through written texts (Greek Linear B, for example), or have an ideographic writing system (the ancient Mayan hieroglyphics, for example). Without the sound system on which all of these writing systems are based, the result would be something not human.

What about deaf-mutes, one wonders? Do they communicate by means of language? We all recognize

that the answer must be yes. While they may not
use sounds in the process of communicating, and
while some signs are international, the vast
majority are heavily dependent upon the specific
language spoken in the community where the deaf-
mute lives. An American deaf-mute cannot fully
communicate with a Spanish deaf-mute through language unless one or the other is bilingual.

Bees communicate with one another through
the well-known "bees' dance," but this communication amazing as it is, is not really comparable
to human language. The attempts in recent years
to teach a communication system to chimpanzees
provide the basis for what could perhaps be
called a "para-language," that is, an artificially
created system based on English morphology
and syntax, which even for the most intelligent
of the chimpanzees, is severely limited by human
comparison. In addition, if the operator of the
machine used by the chimpanzees to form their
sentences didn't understand English, there would
be virtually no communication. Recent studies
in fact have called into question the validity
of the entire experiment.

Language then clearly is a means of communication, but not all means of communication may be
called language. A language must have a system of
sounds in which groups of sounds are formed in a
meaningful pattern within a structure that permits
large numbers of people to communicate freely
about matters both concrete and abstract.

Sign languages and gestures are means of
communication now being studied by that branch of
linguistics known as kinesics, but because the
field is relatively new, a great deal of study
remains to be done. Another very fruitful area
of linguistic study appears to lie in the new
field of machine languages, a study which offers
some prospect of new revelations about languages
and how they work.

LANGUAGE FAMILIES

To gain a broad perspective it is appropriate that we see how Spanish fits into the general classification of the languages of the world.
For centuries, scholars of all nations have been
interested in language classification, but prior
to the nineteenth century, most systems were based
more upon the imagination or the wishes of the
scholar than upon any real relationship with fact.
One well-known example saw the Swede, Andreas
Kemke, hypothesize that in the Garden of Eden,
Adam spoke Danish, the Serpent French, and God
Swedish! The early history of linguistics is
filled with many such misplaced loyalties.

One figure stands out however in the early
history of modern linguistics, Sir William Jones,
a British judge who lived for many years in India
and who spent a profitable period of time study-
ing the documents at his disposal written in Sanskrit, the language of ancient India. In 1786 he
presented his findings in a discourse which was to
lead to the important philological discoveries of
the nineteenth century. In his discourse he
suggested that Greek, Latin and Sanskrit were all
related to some previous, unknown language. Earlier scholars, like the misguided Swede, Kemke,
had always attempted to derive one language from
another contemporary one, like deriving Latin
from Greek, or Spanish from Italian. Jones led
the way out of this fallacious reasoning process,
and laid the groundwork for the discovery of the
ancestor of most of the languages of Europe,
Indo-European.

Jones' hypothesis was later refined by
August Schleicher in the nineteenth century when
he postulated the concept of a FAMILY TREE (árbol
geneológico). In this theory, the parent language (such as Latin for example) has branches
from which spring the daughter languages (such as
Spanish, French, Italian, etc.).

The result of the investigations of several

3

generations of philologists has produced the important model of language relationships which we still use today for explaining the historical differentiation of languages. Using the comparative method and/or the method of internal reconstruction it is possible to reconstruct with a considerable degree of accuracy an ancestor language which is no longer spoken and for which documentary evidence is scanty or nonexistent. The COMPARATIVE METHOD takes evidence from two or more daughter languages and reconstructs the most likely form the ancestor language would have taken. The more documentation available the better and the more reliable the results. Fortunately, the Romance Languages and their ancestor Latin are very well documented. Through INTERNAL RECONSTRUCTION, a synchronic analysis of a language produces evidence which enables us to propound part of the history of that language when used in combination with the widely known historical sound processes that languages undergo.

A synchronic study of a language is one that analyzes the state of a language at a given point in time. A diachronic study examines the language at two or more points in its history. In this book we shall have occasion to deal with both kinds of studies.

In the world today there are vast numbers of language families, among which must be included:

1. INDO-EUROPEAN. This very important family includes most of the languages of Europe including the Romance Languages and the Germanic Languages. Often termed ProtoIndo-European, the proto- prefix means that the language is reconstructed without the benefit of written documentation to verify the findings.

2. HAMITO-SEMITIC. This family includes the Semitic languages of which

4

the most well-known are Arabic and
Hebrew, and the Berber languages of
North Africa as well as Coptic (the
language of the Coptic Church of Egypt)
and Chad (spoken in West Africa).

3. FINNO-UGRIC. A language family of
Europe not related to Indo-European.
It consists primarily of Finnish, Es-
tonian and Lappish.

4. BASQUE. A non-Indo-European language which is related to no other
known language of the world (a condition often described as a "language
isolate"). Basque is important for
our studies because it is one of the
languages spoken in the Iberian
Peninsula (most frequently used in
northern Spain near the Cantabrian Sea
and in southwestern France).

5. Other large language families of the
world include: ALTAIC (the family
which includes Turkic and Mongolian),
CAUCASIAN (divided into Northern and
Southern Caucasian, and containing
many of the languages of the Caucasus
Mountain region of the Soviet Union),
SINO-TIBETAN (including Chinese,
Tibetan and Burmese), DRAVIDIAN
(spoken in parts of India and Malaya),
JAPANESE-KOREAN, and other less
well-known language families.

6. The most important indigenous language families of the Spanish-speaking
part of the New World include:
NAHUATL (the language of the Aztecs
and related tribes in Mexico),
MAYAN (spoken in the Yucatan Peninsula
of Mexico and in parts of Central
America), ARAWAK and CARIB (spoken in
the Caribbean and in northern South

America), QUECHUA (spoken in the Andes
by the Incas and related groups) and
TUPI-GUARANI (spoken in Brazil and
Paraguay).

ROMANCE LANGUAGES FAMILY TREE

The Romance Languages most often discussed
may be diagrammed as in the following representation of the family tree of the ROMANCE LANGUAGES:

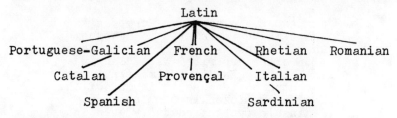

Spanish shares the Iberian Peninsula with Portu-
guese-Galician (gallego-portugués), Catalan
(catalán), and Basque (vasco or vascuence), the
latter once again not an Indo-European language.
The Romance Languages are all derived from
Vulgar Latin and are spoken in those parts of
Europe which once formed the Roman Empire.   The
Roman Empire gave rise to the [Roman]ce Languages.

The study of how Vulgar Latin developed into
the modern Romance Languages is called PHILOLOGY
by some, and HISTORICAL LINGUISTICS by others.
In Europe, philology also encompasses literary
studies, but in our chapter on philology (Chapter
5), we shall restrict our discussion to language
alone, presenting a fairly detailed account of
the most important sound changes which have contributed to the development of the Spanish language.

DIALECTOLOGY

In virtually all the major languages of the
world, as a result of historical development, one
dialect has achieved preeminence over the others,

6

and in those cases where two strong dialects co-
exist over a long period of time, they often become two separate languages. Succinctly put, a
DIALECT is the manner in which one group of
native speakers uses the language. The dialect's
unique manner of speech is usually determined by:
1. Geography (a group isolated from its neighbors
by a river, a mountain range, a political boundary or some other physical obstacle), or 2. So-
cioeconomic class (historically the lower classes have been illiterate, and as a result their
dialect(s) tends to show a more rapid pattern of
change since it has not had the benefit of the
conservative regulator of language found in the
written text).

    DIALECTOLOGY, by extension, is the study of
dialects, and the linguist who studies them is
often called a dialect geographer. Using a map
the dialect geographer draws an isogloss (isoglosa), a line on a map which separates language
usages and which usually shows the pronunciation
of a word or words or the preference for one word
or phrase over another. When several isoglosses,
"bundles" of isoglosses, converge on the same
place, the linguist recognizes that the line
marks a boundary between significant dialect re-
gions.

    Among the most influential and productive
dialects of Spanish are the geographical dialects
of: 1. Castilla, 2. Andalusia, 3. Mexico, 4. Caribbean and Central America, 5. Colombia, 6. Peru,
7. Chile, 8. Argentina. The dialect of Galicia
has close affinity with Portuguese even though
it falls within the political entity of Spain.
Catalan, the language of Catalonia (Cataluña) in
northeastern Spain is usually classified as a
separate Romance language, distinct from Spanish.

    The model for the Spanish used in this
book is a generalized Spanish-American one without the localisms of a particular dialect.
Some dialect variations will be noted as such,
however, in the chapter on phonology.

7

One additional term is appropriate here, the term IDIOLECT, which is the manner of speaking of an individual—the idiosyncracies of speech unique to each person. Occasionally the distinct manner of speaking of an important, influential person is imitated by a large group. This viewpoint led many to believe that the Castilian interdental pronunciation of the letters c in cinco and z in zapato was due to the influence of the Hapsburgs and their hereditary lantern jaw which undoubtedly caused them to speak with a lisp. Most modern linguists discount the importance of this theory, citing evidence that the dialect has resulted from a normal sound-change development.

EXERCISE

1. Which of the following languages are Indo-European and which are not?

      a. Catalan   e. Greek
      b. Polish   f. Hungarian
      c. Swedish   g. Czech
      d. Basque   h. Rhetian

2. Which of the following is not a Romance language?

      a. Sardinian   d. Portuguese
      b. Romanian   e. Provençal
      c. Greek

3. Name and locate the five most important Indian languages spoken in Spanish America.

4. Identify and locate five major dialects of Spanish.

5. Define LINGUISTICS. What is a LANGUAGE? (Derive your own definition and attempt to test it scientifically).

Chapter 1

AN OUTLINE HISTORY OF THE SPANISH LANGUAGE

PRE-ROMAN SETTLEMENT

We know that the Iberian Peninsula has long
been inhabited by man, but we know very little a-
bout the languages spoken there in prehistoric
times. We know that man has flourished through
evidence of artistic achievements, such as the
renowned cave paintings at Altamira (just in-
land from Santillana del Mar on the Cantabrian
coast), which are believed to be at least 12,000
years old.

The earliest linguistic evidence that has
come down to us is very limited, a pair of words,
páramo (a barren landscape) and lama (mud, slime)
a handful of names, Badajoz, Berganza, Carabanzo,
Toledo and Velasco, and the suffix (sufijo),
-asco as in peñasco and nevasca. These are the
only remains we have of the Ligurii, a people who
spoke a non-Indo-European language. We know that
the Ligurii dwelled in the Iberian Peninsula
sometime before 1000 B.C., and that they later
settled in what is now northwestern Italy after
having been displaced by the Celts and the
Iberians.

An ancient group of greater importance to
the history of the Iberian Peninsula as well as
to the Spanish language is that of the Iberians,
a people who gave their name to the Peninsula and
its later inhabitants. There is considerable
discussion about their origin, with the majority
of modern scholars opting for Africa. In recent
years as well, there has been confusion about the
distinction between the Iberians and the Basques,
with some scholars saying that they are unrelated, and others affirming that they are the same.
It is generally conceded now that the Basques are
the surviving heirs of the ancient Iberians and
that their language is related to Iberian in
much the same way that Spanish is related to

9

Latin. We know historically that by 600 B.C. the
Iberians had settled in the Ebro valley and that
they had been there for a considerable time, probably having invaded in large numbers around the
year 1000 B.C. The most important element of
Iberian linguistic influence is the suffix,
-rro/-rra as in, cachorro (puppy, cub), becerro
(calf), perro, guijarro (pebble), garra (claw),
zorro. In addition, other lexical evidence remains: brujo (sorcerer), conejo and manteca
(lard). For Iberian as well as for the other
ancient languages, considerable valuable evidence
is derived from the study of ONOMASTICS, which
among other topics is made up of the study of
place names (TOPONYMY—toponimia) and the study
of personal and family names (PATRONYMICS—patronimia). Toponymy has resulted in giving us the
Iberian words, arroyo and carpio (hill), as well
as the suffix, -berri ("new") used to create
Javier (from Eşaberri meaning "new house") and
Elvira (from Iriberri meaning "new city").

        Another group of great importance in the
history of the Iberian Peninsula was that of the
Celts. Speaking an Indo-European language, they
migrated west through what is now southern France
from Germany, and invaded the Iberian Peninsula
sometime around the ninth century B.C., and again
in the sixth century B.C. In the succeeding
centuries they mixed with the Iberians to form
what is called the CELT-IBERIAN race, the dom-
inant group of the Peninsula at the time of the
Roman invasion. The lexicon of modern Spanish
has been enriched via Latin with several words of
Celtic origin: brío, bragas, cabaña, camisa,
camino, carro, cerveza, gato, legua, plomo,
vasallo. Some place names derive from Celtic
stems: Segovia (from sego meaning "victory" plus
Latin via), and Coimbra (from conim plus briga
which means "fortress").

        In the ancient world, two groups not yet
mentioned were also participants in the life of
the Iberian Peninsula: the Greeks and the
Phoenicians. Both groups were primarily inter-

ested in trade, and the settlements they founded
were mainly limited to coastal cities and towns.
The Phoenicians as well, founded Carthage in the
ninth century B.C., and in their spirit of expansion of trade, Phoenicians and Carthaginians
also founded the Peninsular cities of <u>Gadir</u> (now
<u>Cádiz</u>), and <u>Malaka</u> (now <u>Málaga</u>). Also Phoeni-
cian/Carthaginian is the word, <u>mapa</u>, and the
name, <u>Hispania</u>, which supposedly meant "land of
rabbits." The Greeks colonized the eastern and
northeastern coast, especially the Levantine
coast (from Murcia north). Although no words of
Greek origin have entered Spanish directly from
ancient times, Greek has enriched the Spanish
language in the same way as the other languages
of the ancient world, principally through Latin.
To express it in slightly different terms, the
lexicon of the ancient language (ie. Greek,
Phoenician, Iberian, Celtic) entered Latin in
those situations where Latin had no word of its
own to express the idea or to name the object.
From Latin it later underwent those sound
changes which also acted upon the rest of the
lexicon in its development into Spanish. Some
examples of words of Greek origin which underwent these sound changes include: <u>ancla</u>, <u>baño</u>,
<u>bodega</u>, <u>cada</u>, <u>cámara</u>, <u>cuerda</u>, <u>golpe</u>, <u>huérfano</u>,
<u>orégano</u>, <u>quemar</u>, <u>yeso</u> (gypsum). Perhaps of even
greater importance is that part of the lexicon
dealing with Christianity which is also of Greek
origin: <u>bautizar</u>, <u>biblia</u>, <u>Cristo</u>, <u>iglesia</u>,
<u>obispo</u>, <u>paraíso</u>, <u>tumba</u>. Many modern words are
created from Greek stems as well: <u>teléfono</u>,
<u>fonógrafo</u>, <u>termómetro</u>, <u>psiquiatría</u>, etc.

SUBSTRATUM/SUBSTRATA

The effect of all the pre-Roman languages
on the later development of Vulgar Latin into
Spanish has been described as the influence of
the SUBSTRATUM/SUBSTRATA (SUBSTRATUM = the influence of one language; SUBSTRATA = the influence of two or more languages). The combined
influence of the substrata upon the later development of Spanish may be outlined in this
way:

1. Initial f in Latin develops into aspirated h in early Spanish which then becomes Ø (nothing) in modern Spanish. The
h found in modern spelling is the result of
the orthographic conservatism of writing.
Some examples include: FAGEA>haya, FILIU>
hijo, and FUMO>humo (the > shows development from LATIN into Spanish). This sound
change appears to result from the lack of
initial f in Iberian/Basque, and words beginning with this sound were altered to begin with h, a sound that did exist in the
language of the Iberians. As additional
evidence, it is important to note that this
phenomenon does not occur in any other
Romance Language.

2. Spanish also differs from the other
Romance Languages in that there is confusion
between the articulation of the letter b
(representing a bilabial stop) and the letter v (representing a labiodental fricative)of Latin origin. It is postulated
that this phenomenon is also due to the
influence of the Basques. The precise
manner in which these letters are inter-
preted phonologically in modern Spanish
will be discussed in our chapter on phonology (Chapter 2).

3. A third influence of the substratum
upon Spanish is that of the fricative allophones of the voiced stops, /b/, /d/, and
/g/, in such words as lobo, lodo, and lago.
Spanish is the only Romance language so
affected, and again it is believed to result from the influence of the Basque language which shows evidence of the same phenomenon. A more detailed discussion of how
and when these sounds are articulated may
also be found in our chapter on phonology.

4. The Celtic substratum seems to have
predominated in the sonorization (voicing
of unvoiced sounds) of intervocalic Latin

stops, as for example in AQUA>agua and MATREM>madre. Additional examples and clarification of this sound change may be found in the chapter on philology (Chapter 5) and the chapter on phonology.

5. The fifth example of the influence of the substrata consists of the words of pre-Roman origin which have already been introduced.

By way of a summary, the map below offers a visual outline of several of the most important points.

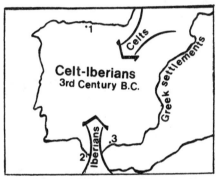

1. Altamira
2. Gadir
3. Malaka

Map 1: Pre-Roman Settlement

ROMAN CONQUEST AND RULE

The rivalry between Rome and Carthage over control of Sicily led to a series of confrontations which grew into a series of three wars which we call the Punic Wars (264-146 B.C.). The power of Rome continued to grow, and Rome emerged victorious from each of the three wars. More importantly from the standpoint of the Iberian Peninsula, these wars were fought in part on Hispanic soil, primarily with the aim

13

of preventing the enemy from controlling it.
Nearly everyone has heard the story of Hannibal
and his elephants who crossed through Hispania,
Gaul and over the Alps, and who almost succeeded
in conquering Rome. It was to prevent such oc-
curences from happening again that the complete
and thorough Roman conquest of the Iberian Peninsula was undertaken. The conquest itself began
in 218 B.C., with Cadiz falling in 206 B.C.,
Numancia in 134 B.C. and the entire Peninsula
finally in 19 B.C. The resistance of Numancia,
coupled with the fact that its inhabitants chose
a final collective suicide rather than acceptance
of Roman rule has long been used to explain and
justify Spanish intransigence.

Because the Iberian Peninsula became part
of the Roman Empire when the power of Rome was
still on the ascent, and because the final conquest was so long lasting and complete, Hispania
became virtually as Roman as Rome itself. The
Latin of Hispania, while differing somewhat from
that of Rome (Roman senators often made fun of
the accents of Iberian writers and representa-
tives), was very conservative and resembled the
Latin of Rome very closely, more closely than
that of any of the territories conquered later.
Hispania in fact became perhaps the favorite
province of the Empire, and as such gave birth
to three emperors, Trajan, Marcus Aurelius, and
Theodosius, and numerous writers, among whom we
note Quintilian, Seneca, Lucan and Martial. In
histories of Spanish literature, this period is
often called the Silver Age (Edad de Plata) because of the great wealth of literary talent.

The Latin which was brought to Hispania
with the conquering Roman soldiers was a somewhat simplified form known commonly as Vulgar
Latin (the spoken Latin of the time). Again,
because the conquest was so complete, the previous languages left virtually no trace of influence on the structure of the spoken Latin of
Hispania. Only those sound changes already mentioned caused the Latin of Hispania to begin

14

developing in its unique path towards Spanish.

It would be possible to devote pages and pages of learned discussion to Classical Latin, Vulgar Latin, how they differed, and how they developed eventually into Spanish. Instead of choosing that course at present, however, let us summarize economically the changes from Classical Latin to Spanish in these nine points:

1. Spanish sees the creation of the definite and indefinite articles (el, la, un, una, etc.) which did not exist in Latin.

2. The Latin system of five declensions is reduced to two (masculine and feminine, bueno, buena).

3. The reduction of grammatical cases from fourteen in Latin to three in Spanish (yo, me, mí; tú, te, ti).

4. Because of the great loss of grammatical cases, Spanish makes use of prepositions to a much greater extent than did Latin.

5. The four conjugations of Latin verbs (-ĀRE, -ĒRE, -ĔRE, -ĪRE) become three in Spanish (-ar, -er, -ir).

6. The ten vowels of Classical Latin (Ā, Ă, Ē, Ĕ, Ī, Ĭ, Ō, Ŏ, Ū, Ŭ) become five in modern Spanish (a, e, i, o, u) together with two diphthongs (discussed in the chapter on philology).

7. The passive voice and future conjugations of Latin are eliminated, and created anew in Spanish through PERIPHERASIS. Instead of CANTABO (I shall sing) Spanish uses cantaré, which has been created from the infinitive cantar plus the helping verb haber, conjugated he. Cantar he has become modern cantaré.

15

<u>8</u>. Spanish sees the introduction of the conditional (<u>amaría</u>) and the perfects (<u>he amado</u>, <u>había amado</u>, etc.).

<u>9</u>. Classical Latin was a quantitative language in which accent was indicated by the length of time a sound was maintained. The use of long and short vowels indicates this quality which we note in: AMĀRE (to love) and AMĀRĒ (bitterly); TERRĀ (land) TERRĀ (by the land). Old English was also a quantitative language, and modern English still bears a closer resemblance to this kind of language system than does modern Spanish which has become a qualitative language wherein accent is shown by intensity (loudness): <u>amara</u> vs. <u>amará</u>, and <u>amo</u> vs. <u>amó</u>. This point will be approached again in our chapter on phonology.

The percentage of Latin influence on the lexicon of Spanish is enormous, with the minimum certainly not less than sixty percent, and a view of as much as eighty percent could probably be defended. A Spanish word list of words of Latin origin could easily contain more pages than this entire book, but as examples of this part of the lexicon, let these suffice:

1. Words which underwent no change at all in becoming Spanish: <u>animal</u>, <u>ante</u>, <u>contra</u>, <u>de</u>, <u>enorme</u>, <u>tarde</u>.

2. Nouns which lost only the final Latin -<u>M</u>: <u>casa</u>, <u>campo</u>, <u>cocina</u>, <u>libro</u>, <u>risa</u>.

3. Verbs which lost only the final -<u>E</u>: <u>amar</u>, <u>cantar</u>, <u>dormir</u>, <u>estar</u>, <u>tener</u>, <u>volver</u>.

4. Numerous popular words were much deformed through progressive sound changes: <u>FACTUM</u>><u>hecho</u>, <u>CIVITATEM</u>><u>ciudad</u>, <u>PAUPEREM</u>> <u>pobre</u>, <u>ALIQUOD</u>><u>algo</u>.

The VISIGOTHS

The period of history known as the Dark Ages
coincides with the period of the westward and
southward expansion of the Germanic tribes, and
the almost simultaneous expansion of the Arabic-
speaking empire. Both events combined to disrupt
the trade of the Mediterranean, and this in turn
deepened the economic depression which characterized the period. Curiously, both movements
of peoples saw their moments of fullest expansion
shortly after having conquered the Iberian
Peninsula.

In the first century after Christ, large
groups of Goths emigrated from Scandinavia, the
two largest being the Visigoths (from what is
now Norway) and the Ostrogoths (from what is
present day Sweden). At first they wandered
southeastward, across the plains (of modern day
Poland and Russia) until they reached Dacia
(present day Hungary). There at the gates of the
Roman Empire they remained long enough to become
converted to Christianity (an Arian sect however,
which was later declared heretical by the Church).
Because of increasing pressure from the east in
the form of the Huns, the Visigoths offered to
become vassals of the Roman Empire and to help
defend against the Huns in return for permission
to cross the Danube and to dwell within the Empire itself. Their offer accepted, in a matter
of only a few years, the weakness of the Empire
became apparent, and to assuage their dissatis-
faction, the Visigoths continued their armed
migration to the south and then west to the
Apenine Peninsula and finally to Rome itself.
The Visigoths, in fact, sacked Rome in 476 A.D.,
a date which many scholars use to signal the fall
of the Roman Empire and the beginning of the Dark
Ages. The Visigoths, not yet satisfied, continued
their migrations north and west to Gaul. There
they settled for a time, sending one group of
warriors ahead into the Iberian Peninsula sometime around the end of the fifth century. A
century later, after having been defeated by the
Franks (another Germanic tribe), the whole of

the Visigothic population crossed the Pyrenees and invaded the Iberian Peninsula in earnest. The Hispano-Romans were soon overrun and the government and nobility fell into the hands of the Goths. There they remained in power until the year 711 when the Arabs made their successful invasion and brought about the defeat of the Gothic kingdom.

In addition to the Visigoths, the Germanic tribes who successfully invaded the Peninsula included the Vandals who gave their name to southern Spain, Andalucia, "land of the Vandals." The Vandals, earliest of the Germanic invaders and pressed by the Visigoths, continued across the Strait of Gibraltar, across North Africa to Tunisia and then to Sicily where they established a Vandal kingdom. An allied tribe of Goths, the Suevians, settled mainly in the northwestern part of Spain, and are said by some linguists to have caused the major part of the differentiation of Galician-Portuguese from Spanish.

We know very few Germanic words which entered directly into the Vulgar Latin of the Peninsula, only: brotar (to sprout, spring forth), espeto (a spit for roasting), hato (ranch), rapar (to shave), tascar (to beat; to chew), and triscar (to mix, mingle).

The lexicon of modern Spanish is rich in words of Germanic origin however, as may be noted in the following groupings of words which entered Latin for the most part prior to the Visigothic invasion of Hispania:

1. Words relating to warfare and horse-manship: aleve (treacherous), ardido (brave, bold), ayo (tutor), bandera, bandido, bando, botín, bramar (to roar, bellow), brida (bridle), dardo (dart, shaft), espía, ganar, guardar, guarnir (to rig), guerra, guía, guisa, hacha, robar, tregua (truce), compañero, espuela, estribo.

18

2. Words relating to feudalism and to certain human qualities: barón, fresco, franco, heraldo, galardón (reward, prize), orgullo, rico, tacaño, and also the suffix -engo, as in abolengo (ancestry), abadengo (abbatial) and realengo (royal lands).

3. Words pertaining to clothing and shelter: albergue (shelter), blanco, falda, guante, ropa, sala, yelmo.

4. Proper names: Alfonso, Alvaro, Bermudo Elvira, Federico, Froilán, Fernando, Gonzalo, Matilde, Ramiro, Ricardo, Rodrigo, etc.

The map included here summarizes the three principal groups of Germanic invaders:

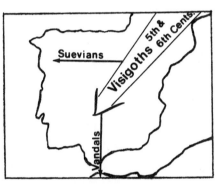

Map 2: Germanic Invasions

The ARABS

According to legend, Spain was lost because Rodrigo, the last of the Visigothic kings, saw a maiden, la Cava, while she was bathing. Smitten with desire he called her to his quarters and made love to her. As a result of her seduction she wrote a letter to her father, conde Julián, the alcalde of Ceupta (a city on the north

19

coast of Africa, just east of the Strait of Gibraltar) and begged that he avenge Rodrigo's act. In response to this letter, conde Julián led Tarif on a reconaissance mission in 710 which revealed how weak Spain was. The next year, 711, Tariq first and Musa later led two fantastically successful invasion forces which quickly overcame all Visigothic resistance. Later Spanish writers attempt to explain the tragedy by imbuing the whole episode with the tone of a reenactment of the loss of paradise in which Rodrigo has the role of Adam, la Cava that of Eve and the apple, and Spain the lost paradise.

Whatever the cause, we know that the conquest of the Iberian Peninsula by the Arabs was vastly successful, and that Arabic-speaking peoples were to remain in control of at least a portion of it from 711 to 1492.

Linguistically speaking, after Latin, the most important influence on Spanish is that of Arabic. Some estimates place the amount of the Spanish lexicon having an Arabic origin at nearly eight percent. The strength of this Arabic component is one of the things which makes Spanish distinct from the other Romance Languages. What is strange about the phenomenon though is not that Arabic has influenced Spanish so much, but that it has influenced Spanish so little. There is no detectible influence of Arabic on Spanish syntax, very little on Spanish morphology (contributing the suffix -í, as in maravedí, alfonsí) and virtually nothing on Spanish pronunciation. This despite the more than 350 years in which Arabic-speaking people controlled more than half of the Peninsula (Toledo was recaptured by the Christians only in 1069). In addition the Arabic language was the principal repository of learning in the Peninsula prior to the eleventh century. In all, the Arabic-speaking people played a prominent role in Spain's history for more than 750 years.

The linguistic contribution of Arabic

to Spanish is almost entirely lexical. Many of
the words are characterized by their curious
redundancy as if the Spaniards didn't understand
Arabic: the prefix al- in Arabic serves as the
definite article, yet the same words in Spanish
are used with a Spanish definite article as
well, almacén ("the warehouse" in Arabic), and
el almacén (redundant, "the the warehouse").
The same thing has happened in English with some
Arabic loan words, algebra, alfalfa, alchemy, but
not as frequently as Spanish, witness the Spanish
versus the English in these examples: azafrán
(saffron), algodón (cotton), azufre (sulphur).
Redundancy in the Spanish borrowings also may
be seen in the use of the prefix guadal- (from
wadi meaning "river") as in Guadalquivir, and
redundant in el Río Guadalquivir.

Nevertheless, the Arabic contribution to
the Spanish lexicon is very large and especially
rich in these areas:

1. Agriculture: alberca (pool, reser-
voir), aceite, aceituna, albaricoque
(apricot), alcachofa (artichoke), alfalfa,
algodón, arroz, azafrán, azúcar, berenjena,
(eggplant), naranja, noria (water wheel),
zanahoria (carrot).

2. Science: alambique (still), alcalí
(alkali), alcohol, algoritmo (logrithm),
álgebra, alquimia, azufre, cenit (zenith)
cifra, elixir, jarabe (syrup), quilate
(carat), redoma (vial).

3. Warfare: alcaíde (governer, warden),
alcazaba (fortress within a walled town),
alcázar, atalaya (watchtower), jinete,
tambor, zaga (rear of an army).

4. Buildings and furnishings: adobe,
alcoba (bedroom), aldea, alfombra, almohada,
azotea (flat roof), azulejo (tile), barrio,
zaguán (vestibule, hallway).

5. Toponymy: <u>Alcalá</u>, <u>Alhambra</u>, <u>la Mancha</u>, <u>Guadalajara</u>, <u>Guadarrama</u>, <u>Guadalquivir</u>.

6. Miscellaneous: <u>ajedrez</u>, <u>alacrán</u>, <u>alcalde</u>, <u>almacén</u>, <u>azul</u>, <u>fulano</u> (SO-and-so), <u>mengano</u> (so-and-SO), <u>jarra</u>, <u>jazmín</u>, <u>ojalá</u>, <u>tarea</u>.

At the time of the invasion, the Visigoths were so utterly defeated that they were forced to flee from the battlefields. A handful of Goths (godos) under the leadership of Pelayo took refuge in the cave at Covadonga, and there managed to hold off the attackers in 718. This date marks the beginning of the Reconquista in Spain (even though the Arabs continued into France and were halted only in 732 at Poitiers, France), which was to end only in 1492 with the surrender of Granada to the Reyes Católicos. The map below indicates the major moments of Islamic civilization in Spain.

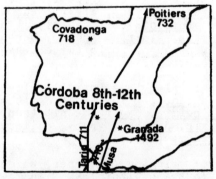

Map 3: Arabic Spain

MEDIEVAL SPAIN

The dialect of Spanish which came to dominate in the development of modern Spanish is

the dialect of Castilla which had both conservative and advanced tendencies in the Middle Ages.
It was conservative in that its lexicon changed
more slowly than that of some of the other dialects,
and more advanced in its sound changes. The
stressed vowels of Vulgar Latin more regularly
diphthongized in Castellano, especially open-e
which diphthongized to ie in modern Spanish, as
in SEPTEM>siete, and open-o which became the
diphthong ue as in BONUM>bueno (a much more complete discussion of this phenomenon may be found
in our chapter on philology).

One may wonder why it is that Castellano
is the dialect which attained dominance? The
answer involves recalling certain aspects of
Spanish civilization. For most of the Middle
Ages, Castilla was the frontier battleground
of the Iberian Peninsula, and as such attracted
most of the young men who sought to advance
themselves. There, during some four hundred
years (850-1250), they could obtain wealth, glory
and fame through feats of arms. A very well
known example of this may be seen in the struggles
of Rodrigo Díaz de Vivar as glorified especially
in the Poema de Mio Cid. Castilla itself, composed of Castilla la Vieja and Castilla la Nueva,
grew in size and power and saw itself for most of
the late Middle Ages the seat of the most power-
ful military kingdom of the Peninsula.

Its importance was consolidated as it became the dialect most often used in literary
works, such as Berceo's Milagros de Nuestra
Señora, the Libro de Alexandre, and other such
medieval masterpieces. The most important
benefactor for the eventual dominance of Castellano, however, was Alfonso X, el Sabio, who
ruled from 1252 to 1284. It was his decision to
write in Castellano the important and well-known
histories, Primera crónica general de España,
the General estoria, the fundamental legal trea-
tise of the Middle Ages, the Siete partidas, and
the other books he sponsored which contained
much of the scientific knowledge of his day,

Lapidario, Libro de astronomía, and others. His
immense and lovely collection of miracles of the
Virgin, Cántigas de Santa María, was written in
Gallego-portugués, the language of the Peninsula
most often used by the Iberian troubadours for
their lyrical efforts.

The final consolidation of Spain was brought
about during the reign of the Reyes Católicos after
Fernando of Aragón joined Isabel of Castilla and
León in matrimony. Their reign also saw the
ultimate defeat of the Moors when Granada was
finally taken in 1492, the year of the simultaneous discovery of the New World.

The NEW WORLD

Of very great importance for Spain and also
for the development of the Spanish language was
the discovery of the New World. Not only were
immense riches of gold, silver and other precious
items brought back from the New World, but also
the words needed to name the flora, fauna and
customs found there.

As might be expected, the largest groups
of Indians contributed a good many words, but what
might seem surprising at first glance is that the
group which provided the largest number were the
Indians of the Caribbean. It is surprising because these Indians have now ceased to exist for
the most part, having succumbed to disease, warfare and slavery. Despite this, because they were
the first Indians who had close contact with the
Spaniards, a monument remains to them in the
lexicon of modern Spanish which has carried their
terminology throughout the Spanish-speaking world,
and includes these words among others: ají
(chili), barbacoa, banana, cacique, caimán (alli-
gator), caníbal, canoa, caoba, cayo (key, string
of islands), ceiba (type of tree), guano (palm
tree), hamaca, henequén, huracán, iguana, maíz,
maguey, nigua (chigger), plátano, sábana, tabaco,
tiburón (shark), tuna (prickly pear), yuca. From
this small sampling one can easily see that the

24

the words in large part describe plants, animals and artifacts associated with the New World.

The same generalization may also be made about the second largest contribution, that of the Nahuatl-speaking Indians of central Mexico. Some sample words of Nahuatl origin include: aguacate (avocado), cacao, cacahuete (peanut), camote (sweet potato), chicle, chamaco (boy), chocolate, frijol, guajolote (turkey), nopal (cactus), pulque (the milky, fermented cactus juice beverage), tamal, tomate, zopilote (buzzard).

A third group of importance is that of the Quechua-speaking Indians of the Andes. Some words having a Quechua origin include: alpaca, coca (cocaine), cóndor, llama, mate (the beverage), pampa, puma, papa (potato).

The final group which we shall mention is that of the Araucan Indians of Chile. Their contribution to standard Spanish includes at least the words gaucho and poncho.

The word, patata (potato), seems to be a new word created in Spanish by combining the Caribbean word, batata (sweet potato), with the Quechua word, papa.

Other Indian languages of the New World continue producing lexicon used by local Spanish-American dialects, but few of these words are as generally recognized by all Spanish-speaking peoples as the words we have included in this brief discussion. Two large groups of Indians especially influential today are the Mayan Indians of southern Mexico and Guatemala, and the Guaraní Indians of Paraguay.

The Spanish of the New World today differs somewhat from that of Castilla in two main areas: 1. Lexicon (including the influence of the Indian substrata as well as the wide-spread use of the voseo); 2. Pronunciation (including the seseo, the pronunciation of the letters c of cero and z

25

of zona as if they were written with an s. While
there is much discussion of how this came to be,
the general consensus today is that it results
from the high percentage of Andalusians who emigrated early to the New World—the Andalusian
dialect also makes use of the seseo. Spanish-
American also is characterized by extensive use
of the phenomenon known as yeísmo—the pronunciation of the ll as a y).

ITALIAN

The sixteenth century saw Spain's power
expand not only in the New World but in the Old
as well. A great part of the Italian Peninsula
came under Spanish rule, and several small wars
were waged in Italy with Spanish troops under
the command of Carlos V.

Through close and continuing contact for
more than a century with Italian culture, the
Spanish lexicon borrowed a great deal, influenced
to no small degree by the Italian Renaissance.
Most of the loan words fall into these categories:

1. Music: alto, aria, bajo (bass), cantina,
carnaval, compositor, dúo, libreto, madrigal,
soprano, tenor.

2. Literature: gaceta, lira, novela,
soneto, terceto.

3. Art: arabesco, charlatán, claroescuro
(chiaroscuro—treatment of light and dark in
painting), fachada (facade), medalla, modelo,
mosaico, porcelana, terracota, diletante.

4. Warfare, especially naval warfare:
bergantín, brújula (compass), carabina,
centinela, coronel, emboscada, fragata,
escopeta, galera, góndola, piloto, pistola.

SEVENTEENTH CENTURY

From the defeat of the Spanish Armada (1588)

to the death of Calderón de la Barca (1680),
Spain's role as a world power gradually was
dissipated. Even so, it is the period known to
literary scholars as the Golden Age, when Spanish
became the vehicle for the best and most important
literary works in the world (English scholars
might disagree with this evaluation however).
These years saw the production of the unique
contributions of Cervantes, Lope de Vega, Tirso
de Molina, Calderón de la Barca, Quevedo and
Góngora and many others. It is the time of the
glorification and elaboration in literature and
art known often as the Baroque. Artists and
writers of the age endeavored to blend traditional
modes with individual attempts to convey new,
startling or unusual ideas. It is a period filled
with dynamism, doubt and dualities. But most of
all it is the "Spanish Century" when linguistic,
literary and artistic influence was flowing from
Spain to the rest of the world. For this reason,
at this time there is little influence from other
languages on Spanish.

FRENCH

The eighteenth century brought a change in
the ruling family of Spain. The Hapsburgs ruled
Spain from 1517 to 1700, from Carlos V, known in
Spain as Carlos I de España (ruled 1517-56) to
Carlos II (ruled 1665-1700). The Hapsburgs ceased
being the ruling family when Felipe de Anjou was
named by Carlos II as heir to the throne. In
Spain he becomes Felipe V, and is the first of
the kings of the Casa de Borbón, the royal house
of France. As might be expected, this brings
about a long period of close contact between
France and Spain at a time when the power of
France was on the ascent.

Traditionally the eighteenth century has
been viewed as a great void in Spanish literature
and art, but this polemical view is being chal-
lenged somewhat by scholars today. It is an
important time in architecture (the neo-classical
style) when the Prado was constructed, and the

Royal Academies of the Spanish Language and of
History were founded, and the Biblioteca Nacional
was first established.

French contributions to the Spanish language
find considerable acceptance during the eighteenth
century and some acceptance through the nineteenth
and twentieth as well. A list of Spanish words
having a French origin reveals terms mainly related to:

1. Fashion and fashionable actions: blusa,
coqueta, chaqueta, dama, corsé, bisutería
(imitation jewelry), etiqueta, pantalón,
perfume, reloj, silueta, tisú, tupé.

2. Occupation, food and lodgings: bufete,
café, consomé, croqueta, chófer, chalé(t),
filete, gañán (farmhand), garaje, hotel
jaula, jardín, manjar (a special dish),
menú, merengue, paje (page), restaurante,
sargento.

3. Inventions and other French phenomena:
automóvil, avalancha, bajel (vessel, ship),
bayoneta, cofre, cupé, cupón, mamá, papá,
sofá.

4. Fixed phrases: al natural, hacer el
amor, hombre de mundo.

French influence continues even today,
albeit not as strongly as in previous centuries,
having surrendered first place to English.

ENGLISH

The English language has become the world's
primary means of communication in the twentieth
century. The rise to power of Great Britain and
the United States has brought about the current
preponderance of English as the largest source
of words being introduced into Spanish. The
English contributions mainly pertain to:

28

1. Sports: <u>baloncesto</u> ("basketball" in Spain), <u>básquet(bol)</u> or <u>básket</u>, <u>balompié</u>, <u>béisbol</u>, <u>boxeo</u>, <u>esquiar</u>, <u>fútbol</u>, <u>golf</u>, <u>tenis</u>; possibly as well <u>jol</u> (hole), <u>bol</u>, <u>gol</u>.

2. Inventions (many created from Greek stems, but borrowed by Spanish from English): <u>dacrón</u>, <u>fotografía</u>, <u>nilón</u>, <u>radio</u>, <u>rayón</u>, <u>teléfono</u>, <u>telégrafo</u>, <u>telegrama</u>, <u>televisión</u>.

3. Other: <u>bar</u>, <u>club</u>, <u>cheque</u>, <u>control</u>, <u>dándy</u>, <u>detective</u>, <u>dólar</u>, <u>flirtear</u>, <u>líder</u>, <u>revólver</u>, <u>supermercado</u>, <u>sexi</u> or <u>sexy</u>.

In addition there is a penchant in Spain and in many parts of Spanish America for "exotic" English names, as for example the well-known restaurants in Madrid, <u>Nebraska</u> and <u>California</u>. Known throughout the world furthermore are the beverages <u>Pepsi Cola</u> and <u>Coca Cola</u> as well as other well known American products.

Some knowledge of English has become so commonplace in Spain and the Spanish-speaking world that there is some discussion of a newly created class of plurals (morphologically conditioned—see our chapter on morphology, Chapter 3, for a more complete discussion) for the words, <u>jeep</u>, <u>clip</u> and <u>rock</u>. According to the rules of normal Spanish morphology, the plural forms of these nouns would be *<u>jeepes</u>, *<u>clipes</u> and *<u>rockes</u> (the * indicates a non-documented or non-standard form), but knowledge of English has become so pervasive that the expected plurals are: <u>jeeps</u>, <u>clips</u>, and <u>rocks.</u>

SPANISH INFLUENCE on ENGLISH

As a further demonstration of the way that languages borrow vocabulary from other languages, let us note briefly some of the lexicon which English has borrowed from Spanish. The most productive areas are:

1. Toponymy: <u>A</u>rizona, <u>C</u>alifornia, <u>C</u>olorado, Florida, <u>Los Angeles</u>, <u>M</u>ontana, <u>San Antonio</u>, <u>San Diego</u>, <u>San Francisco</u>, <u>T</u>exas, <u>T</u>oledo, etc.

2. Geographical features: <u>arroyo</u>, <u>canyon</u>, <u>hurricane</u>, <u>key</u> (from <u>cayo</u>, a string of is-islands), <u>mesa</u>, <u>mezquite</u>, <u>Pampas</u>, <u>presidio</u>, <u>ranch</u>, <u>savanna(h)</u>, <u>sierra</u>, <u>tornado</u>.

3. Animals: <u>alligator</u> (from <u>el lagarto</u>), <u>alpaca</u>, <u>bronco</u>, <u>burro</u>, <u>condor</u>, <u>coyote</u>, <u>cockroach</u>, <u>iguana</u>, <u>jaguar</u>, <u>llama</u>, <u>mustang</u>, <u>pinto</u>, <u>puma</u>, <u>vicuña</u>.

4. Customs, occupations of the Southwest, and other cultural phenomena: <u>barbecue</u>, <u>bonanza</u>, <u>booby</u> (from <u>bobo</u>), <u>calaboose</u> (from <u>calabozo</u>), <u>cannibal</u>, <u>canoe</u>, <u>chaps</u> (from <u>chaparejos</u>), <u>cinch</u>, <u>corral</u>, <u>desperado</u>, <u>guerrilla</u>, <u>hacienda</u>, <u>hammock</u>, <u>hombre</u>, <u>hoosegow</u> (from <u>juzgado</u>), <u>huaraches</u>, <u>junta</u>, <u>machismo</u>, <u>macho</u>, <u>patio</u>, <u>pecadillo</u>, <u>peon</u>, <u>lasso</u> (from <u>lazo</u>), <u>renegade</u>, <u>rodeo</u>, <u>sherry</u> (from <u>Jerez</u>), <u>siesta</u>, <u>stevedore</u>, <u>vamoose</u>. Included here as well should be the phrase <u>fifth column</u> meaning, "a subversive group working within a given country or city to give aid to an opposing army." The term was coined as the result of a message sent to Madrid in 1936 by General Emilio Mola informing the city that he had four columns surrounding the city and the <u>fifth column</u> of Franco sympathizers within the city itself.

5. Vegetable products: <u>alfalfa</u>, <u>banana</u>, <u>chocolate</u>, <u>cocoa</u>, <u>cacao</u>, <u>cocaine</u>, <u>frijoles</u>, <u>henequen</u>, <u>indigo</u>, <u>maize</u>, <u>marijuana</u>, <u>potato</u>, <u>sassafras</u>, <u>tapioca</u>, <u>tobacco</u>, <u>cigar</u>, <u>tomato</u>, <u>vanilla</u>.

EXERCISE

1. Which of the following are examples of sub-stratum in Spanish?

30

```
a.___   -eta
b.___   f>h>∅
c.___   -í
d.___   -engo
e.___   -rro/-rra
```

2. What is the language of origin of these words?

```
a. Hispania _____    f. ojalá _____
b. cerveza  _____    g. padre _____
c. yelmo    _____    h. pistola _____
d. automóvil_____    i. flirtear_____
e. cóndor   _____    j. tomate _____
```

3. Name the most important changes in the development of Latin into Spanish.

4. Compare and contrast the lexicon in Spanish derived from Italian, French and English.

5. In a good etymological dictionary, look up the origins of these words: izquierdo, truhán, ángel, colocar, banco, acequia, ocelote, caoba, balcón, flan, cóctel.

6. Compare and contrast the Arabic and Germanic contributions to the Spanish lexicon.

SELECTED BIBLIOGRAPHY

Alonso, Amado. Estudios lingüísticos: Temas españoles (Madrid: Gredos, 1967).

Corominas, Joan. Breve diccionario etimológico de la lengua castellana, 2d ed. (Madrid: Gredos, 1967).

Entwistle, William J. The Spanish Language Together with Portuguese Catalan and Basque (1936 rpt. London: Faber & Faber, 1969).

Lapesa, Rafael. Historia de la lengua española (Madrid: Escelicer, 1959).

Menéndez Pidal, Ramón. Manual de gramática

  histórica española (Rpt. Madrid: Espasa-
  Calpe, 1968).

Spaulding, Robert K. How Spanish Grew (Berkeley:
  U. of Calif. P., 1943).

Chapter 2

INTRODUCTION TO SPANISH PHONOLOGY

INTRODUCTION

In this chapter on <u>phonology</u> (fonología),
the study of the sound system of a language,
we shall examine in considerable detail both
Spanish and English. Careful attention to the
content of this chapter should enable one to
recognize and to produce a more native-like
pronunciation. It will also provide a set of
technical data that can be used effectively by
all those wishing to continue their study of
Spanish linguistics.

In the general introduction we noted that
all languages are based upon a sound system of
meaningful sound patterns. These patterns come
in two classes: <u>segmental features</u> (elementos
segmentales) which are the articulated sounds,
and <u>suprasegmental features</u> (elementos suprasegmentales) which are conveyed by intonation
patterns. In this chapter, both classes will
be studied.

The two classes of sound patterns are derived from <u>minimal pairs</u> (cotejos), by which we
establish meaningful differences through assembling
two patterns which are identical except for a
single sound contrast, such as: <u>pato</u> and <u>Paco</u>,
<u>mesa</u> and <u>misa</u>, <u>amo</u> and <u>amó</u>. All three examples
are minimal pairs and demonstrate that the single
difference in sound each pair exemplifies is
important. By the use of minimal pairs, it is
possible to establish all the meaningful sounds
of a language (these meaningful distinctions in
sound are called <u>phonemes</u>—fonemas).

To express the concept in a different way,
the PHONEME is a family of meaningful sounds
used by a language, the members of which may be
exchanged with one another without changing the
meaning of the utterance. Using the inappropri-
ate member will be noticed as unusual by a native

speaker, but the meaning of the utterance will
be conveyed. In this description of phoneme, the
members of the phoneme family are known as
ALLOPHONES (alófonos). The phoneme is the ideal
sound (somewhat akin to that of family name,
like González, Pérez or Herrera) while the allophone is the actual sound produced in an utterance
(akin to the individual members of a family—
Juan González, Pedro González or Enrique González).
In this manner, the English /p/ as an example of
a phoneme (family), has three allophones which
may be noted in these three words: pot, spot,
and top. While all three allophones are distinct
phonetically, they may be exchanged with one
another without changing the meaning of the
utterance even though a native-speaker of English
would recognize a strangeness in the sound if
the wrong allophone were produced.

SEGMENTAL PHONEMES

The segmental phonemes of both Spanish and
English may be divided into four general categories: vowels (las vocales), semivowels (las
semivocales), consonants (las consonantes), and
semiconsonants (las semiconsonantes).

The VOWELS are characterized by a vibration of the vocal cords (las cuerdas vocales)
and the virtually unhindered but shaped passage
of the stream of air (the mouth shapes the air
stream without slowing it or impeding it).

SEMIVOWELS are the second part of diphthongs (diptongos) that begin with vowels, or
the final part of triphthongs (triptongos).
A semivowel is sometimes called an off-glide
(distensión) because it is that part of the
diphthong which is becoming less vowel-like.
An off-glide in English is the last sound in the
word shoe [šu^W], and in Spanish the last sound
in the word hay [ai].

The CONSONANTS are characterized by articulation (articulación), an obstruction of the air
stream which may include among other things:

34

stopping it momentarily, causing it to rub against a part of the mouth, and/or causing it to pass through the nasal passage (la cavidad nasal).

SEMICONSONANTS, sometimes called <u>on-glides</u> (intensión), are the initial parts of diphthongs that end in vowels, or initial parts of triphthongs. An example of a semiconsonant in English is the first part of the triphthong following the <u>v</u> in the word <u>view</u> [vyu^W], and in Spanish the first sound after the <u>p</u> in <u>piel</u> [pyel].

In order to produce all these segmental phonemes, it is necessary to utilize a great part of the upper body: 1. The <u>respiratory organs</u> (los órganos de respiración), 2. The <u>voice producing organs</u> (los órganos de fonación), and 3. The <u>articulatory apparatus</u> (los órganos de articulación).

1. The respiratory organs most necessary in the production of speech sounds include the lungs, the bronchial passages and the traquea.

2. The vocal cords, upon vibrating produce sound which linguists refer to technically as <u>voice</u> or <u>voicing</u> (sonoridad, sonido sonoro, cualidad sonora). If the vocal cords do not vibrate, the sound is considered <u>voiceless</u> or <u>unvoiced</u> (sonido sordo, cualidad sorda).

3. The articulatory apparatus contains organs which are movable as well as those which are used passively. The movable organs include: lips, tongue, lower jaw, velum or soft palate, uvula, pharynx and the epiglottis. The passive organs include the teeth, the alveolar ridge and the hard palate.

A visual display of these features may be seen in the diagram which is reproduced on the next page:

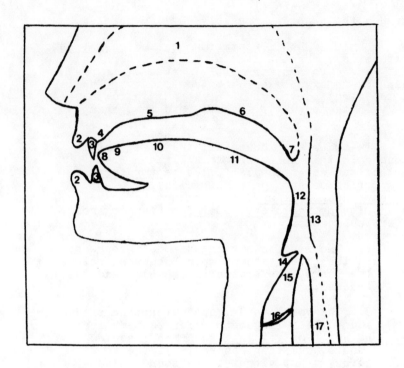

1. Nasal cavity (cavidad nasal)
2. Lips (labios)
3. Teeth (dientes)
4. Alveolar ridge (los alvéolos)
5. Hard palate (paladar)
6. Velum or soft palate (velo)
7. Uvula (úvula)
8. Tip or apex of the tongue (el ápice)
9. Blade (lámina)
10. Center (centro)
11. Dorsum or back of the tongue (dorso)
12. Pharyngeal cavity
13. Pharynx (faringe)

36

14. Epiglottis (epiglotis)
15. Glottis (glotis)
16. Vocal cords (cuerdas vocales)
17. Esophagus (esófago)

CONSONANTS

With this preliminary information about
segmental phonemes and the articulatory apparatus in mind, we may begin our discussion of
the consonants. In English, the linguistic
description of consonants customarily follows
a three-fold descriptive pattern while there
is a four-fold one in Spanish. Both systems
have advantages and disadvantages, and since
they are commonly found, it will be of value
to become familiar with both. We will arrange
them side by side for easy comparison. The
generative pattern of plus and minus features
will be introduced later in this chapter.

In describing ENGLISH CONSONANTS we will
use these three features:

1. Voicing. A consonant will either be
voiced or voiceless (unvoiced).

2. Point or place of articulation. The
consonant may be bilabial, alveolar, velar,
etc., depending on where in the mouth it
is made.

3. Manner of articulation. The way the
consonant is made, whether it be a stop,
a fricative, an affricate or whatever.

The English t in stop for example is: 1. Voiceless,
2. Alveolar, 3. Stop.

In describing SPANISH CONSONANTS we will
follow this four point system:

1. Punto de articulación (point of articulation). Sometimes also called lugar de
articulación.

37

2. **Modo** _de_ __articulación__ (manner of articulation).

3. **Cualidad** _nasal_ u __oral/bucal__ (nasal or
non-nasal).

4. **Sonido** _sonoro_ o __sordo__ (voicing).

The Spanish _t_ in __estar__ is: 1. __(Apico)dental__,
2. __Oclusivo__, 3. __Oral__, 4. __Sordo__. From this point
on, we shall describe the consonants without
using the numbers which have been given here
only to establish the slot order.

STOPS

The first set of consonant phonemes we
shall examine are the STOPS (los oclusivos),
characterized by a momentary stoppage of the
air stream which is then released in a sudden
rush. Because of the nature of this rush of air,
these sounds have sometimes been known as plo-
sives.

In our discussion of the stops, as in all
future discussions of consonant phonemes, the
Spanish phonemes and allophones will be listed
on the left, and English on the right. Descriptions of Spanish consonants will be given in
Spanish, and descriptions of English consonants
will be given in English. For both languages,
phonemes will be indicated by slashes / /, and
allophones by brackets [ ].

OCLUSIVOS	STOPS
/p/, /b/, /t/, /d/, /k/, /g/.	/p/, /b/, /t/, /d/, /k/, /g/.

FONEMA /p/	PHONEME /p/
Un alófono [p]	Three allophones [p^h], [p], [p$^\urcorner$]
[p] palo, pelo, pila, apuesto, popa	[p^h] point, puff, pull

Bilabial, oclusivo,
oral, sordo.

The Spanish [p] is
never aspirated, and
because of this
English-speakers
must learn not to make
the English aspirated
[pʰ] in Spanish words
beginning with a p
followed by a vowel.

Voiceless, bilabial, as-
pirated, stop.

The explosive rush of air
after an initial p in
English is called aspira-
tion.

[p]   spin, supper, spun

Voiceless, bilabial, stop.

[p˥]   slip, snap

Voiceless, bilabial,
unreleased stop.

This allophone is optional
before a pause when the
lips do not open to re-
lease the air.

FONEMA /b/

    Dos alófonos
    [b], [ƀ]

[b]   banco, burro,
      verdad, hambre,
      vuelto, invierno

Bilabial, oclusivo,
oral, sonoro.

Occurs after a pause
or a nasal.

[ƀ]   lobo, abre, lava,
      leve, nube, ave,
      alba, servir

Bilabial, fricativa
oral, sonoro.

PHONEME /b/

    One allophone [b]

[b]   babe, imbibe, brave

Voiced, bilabial stop.

Occurs in all other posi-
tions

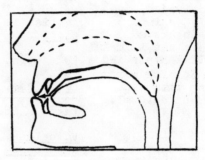

Alófono [b]

     The second allophone of the fonema /b/ in
Spanish is a fricative. By <u>fricative</u> (fricativa)
we indicate that the air stream is impeded in
some manner but not stopped—here impeded by the
two lips which are tense but not quite closed,
as if one were playing the trumpet. It is a
problem sound for speakers of English, because
it represents a new sound to learn. Also compli-
cating the matter is the fact that this fricative
allophone is by far the more common in a normal
utterance. Yet another complication comes from
the education of many speakers of Spanish where
they learn that in many languages the letter <u>v</u> is
labiodental. By analogy, they assume that
"correct" usage is to pronounce the letter <u>v</u>
as a labiodental in <u>vivo</u>, <u>ven</u>, <u>vaya</u>, etc., but
in rapid or careless speech this pronunciation
is seldom maintained. Language usage of the
latter type is frequently described by linguists
as <u>hypercorrection</u> (ultracorrección).

     In order for the English-speaking student
to be able to employ the two allophones of the
/b/ correctly, it is helpful to practice several
exercises like the one we include here:

<u>Oclusivo</u>   <u>Fricativa</u>

Voy   Me voy

bulto	el bulto
vacas	las vacas
vez	la vez
un villano	el villano
un barco	el barco
sin blanca	mi blanca

FONEMA /t/

PHONEME /t/

Un alófono [t̪]

[t̪] tapa, entierro, altar, lata, tomate

(Apico)dental, oclusivo oral, sordo. The comma under the t [t̪] indicates that the sound is dental. It is important to note that Spanish t differs from English in that it is dental not alveolar. The tip of the tongue must touch the back of the upper teeth, as in the diagram below. Substitution of an English t in some situations will cause serious confusion and a failure to communicate. Special difficulty occurs when the speaker of English substitutes the English allophone [r] for the Spanish [t̪] in in words such as lata, pata and nota, because they will be confused with Lara, para,

Three allophones [tʰ], [r], [t]

[tʰ] take, tough, top

Voiceless, alveolar aspirated stop.

Occurs initially when followed by a vowel.

---

[r] water, butter, flatter

Voiced, alveolar flap (or tap).

Occurs commonly in most dialects of American English, between vowels, especially immediately following the stressed vowel. Sometimes called "voiced-t" and transcribed [t̬].

---

[t] lasting, steak, stout

Voiceless, alveolar stop.

Occurs in all other positions.

41

and <u>Nora</u>.

Alófono [t̪]

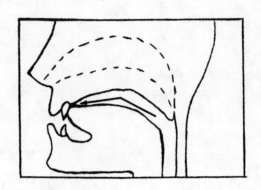

FONEMA /d/

        Dos alófonos
        [d̪], [đ]

[d̪] donde, duro,
      andando,
      falda

(<u>Apico)dental</u>, <u>oclusivo</u>
<u>oral</u>, <u>sonoro</u>.

Occurs after a pause,
a nasal or a lateral.
The comma again in-
dicates a dental sound.

[đ] ardid, verdad,
cuidado, lodo

<u>Interdental</u>, <u>fricativo</u>,
<u>oral</u>, <u>sonoro</u>.

Occurs in all other
positions.

PHONEME /d/

        Two allophones [d], [r]

[r] today, ladder,
     feeder, Friday

<u>Voiced</u>, <u>alveolar</u> <u>flap</u> (or
<u>tap</u>).

The same pattern of distribution as the voiced
allophone of the /t/.

[d] dusted, folded,
     ended

<u>Voiced</u> <u>alveolar</u> <u>stop</u>.

Occurs in all other
positions.

    English-speaking students have two problems
with the Spanish /d/. The student must learn to
articulate the stop allophone as a dental instead

42

of the alveolar which is normal in English. The
second problem is learning to associate the Spanish
spelling system using the d (in lodo or nada) with
a sound similar to one that exists in English, but
which is represented graphically in a different
manner (usually as th in the and father). Both
allophones of the Spanish /d/ require considerable
practice to make correct articularion a habit.
Substitution of an English d [r] for a Spanish
one in lodo would cause it to be heard as loro,
and would not convey the message desired.

Alófono [đ]

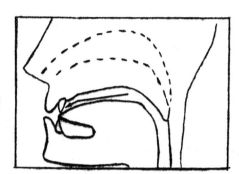

As with the two allophones of the Spanish /b/,
it is helpful when practicing the two allophones
of the Spanish /d/ to make use of several exercises like the one below:

Oclusivo	Fricativa
un duro	dos duros
senda	seda
con Dios	adiós
al día	hoy día
Dora	adora

FONEMA /k/   PHONEME /k/

    Un alófono [k]   Two allophones
                                [kʰ], [k]
[k]   crac, quebrar,

43

Chapúltepec, conozco, quiso

[kʰ] case, king, cow

(Dorso)velar, oclusivo, oral, sordo.

Voiceless, velar aspirated stop.

Occurs in all positions. This sound is like the English /k/ in most situations. Initial [k] however must be practiced to avoid the aspiration of the English allophone.

Occurs initially when followed by a vowel.

[k] faker, skunk, like

Voiceless, velar stop.

Occurs in all other positions.

FONEMA /g/

PHONEME /g/

Dos alofonos [g], [ǥ]

One allophone [g]

[g] gringo, tengo, gula, gota

[g] goggles, pagan, bag

Voiced velar stop.

(Dorso)velar, oclusivo, oral, sonoro.

Occurs after a pause or a nasal.

[ǥ] cargar, hago, zigzag, lagarto

(Dorso)velar, fricativo, oral, sonoro.

Occurs in all other positions.

The fricative allophone of the Spanish /g/ represents a sound that is rarely heard in most dialects of American English (a groan or moan written colloquially as argh! sometimes contains the sound). One must learn to raise the back of the tongue (the dorsum) to a point where it nearly touches the velum and there to constrict the passage of air as though gargling. It is

one of the more difficult of Spanish sounds for
the English-speaking person to make. Inability
to produce this sound will cause a strong accent
but usually will not cause misunderstanding.

Alófono [g]

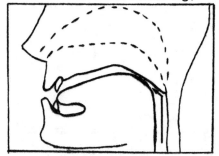

Let us once again offer a sample exercise
which may be used to practice distinguishing the
fricative and stop allophones of the Spanish
/g/.

Oclusivo	Fricativa
grande	Es grande
con gloria	la gloria
tango	Talgo
gato	mi gato
con gota	la gota

DISCUSSION OF STOPS

In general because English has two allophones
for each <u>voiceless</u> stop, an aspirated one and a
non-aspirated one, it is necessary to learn to
avoid aspirating these stops in Spanish when they
occur initially followed by a vowel. At the same
time one must learn to produce a new sound, the
[t] as a dental, not an alveolar as in English.
It is especially important to avoid using the
voiced alveolar flap as an allophone of the
Spanish /t/ in words like <u>foto</u>, and <u>pato</u> because
they will be misunderstood (possibly as <u>foro</u> and
<u>paro</u>).

With regard to <u>voiced</u> stops in Spanish,
because of English habits, many tend to make the
English stop allophones in places where the
Spanish allophones should be fricative. This
clearly is one of the problem areas for students
of Spanish, for mistakes here also tend to cause
considerable misunderstanding. <u>Seda</u> may be heard
as <u>cera</u>, and <u>todo</u> as <u>toro</u>. The fricative [đ]
on the other hand, is easy for the English-speaking
person to articulate because it is very similar
to a phoneme of English (the <u>th</u> in <u>mother</u>, <u>southern</u>,
<u>lather</u>), but requires practice in associating it
with the Spanish /d/. The fricative [g] and the
fricative [b] are sounds which are new—one must
learn to distinguish them and to articulate them
regularly in those situations which call for
their use. This is especially important because
the fricative allophones of the voiced stops are
by far the more frequently used allophones,
and failure to articulate them correctly creates
a rather heavy foreign accent and often entails
a failure to communicate.

FRICATIVES

We shall now take up a second group of
consonants, the <u>fricatives</u> (fricativas), sounds
which are made by constricting or impeding the
air passage in such a way that a friction is
caused that produces meaningful sounds. The
first and last sounds of the words <u>fechas</u> and
<u>jarchas</u>, are fricatives.

FRICATIVAS

/f/, /θ/, /s/, /x/

FRICATIVES

/f/, /v/, /θ/, /đ/
/s/, /z/, /š/, /ž/

The first four are often
called <u>slit</u> <u>fricatives</u> and
the second four, <u>groove</u>
<u>fricatives</u>.

FONEMA /f/

Dos alófonos
[f], [v]

PHONEME /f/

One allophone [f]

46

[v] afgano, Afganistán

Labiodental, fricativa, oral, sonoro.

Rare—occurs before voiced fricative.

[f] faro, Rafael, rosbif

Labiodental, fricativa, oral, sordo.

Occurs in all other positions.

FONEMA /θ/ (in Spain)

Dos alófonos [θ], [z]

[z] juzgado, házmelo

Interdental, fricativa, oral, sonoro.

Occurs before voiced consonant. This allophone contrasts with [ð] only in that it is slightly more interdental.

[θ] gracias, zapato, faz

Interdental, fricativa, oral, sordo.

Occurs in all other positions.

[f] fine, leafing, safe

Voiceless, labiodental fricative.

Occurs in all positions.

PHONEME /v/

One allophone [v]

[v] vine, leaving, save

Voiced, labiodental fricative.

Occurs in all positions.

PHONEME /θ/

One allophone [θ]

[θ] thigh, ether, teeth

Voiceless, interdental fricative.

PHONEME /ð/

One allophone [ð]

[ð] thy, either, teethe

Voiced interdental fricative.

Occurs in all positions.

While both Spanish and English make some use of labiodental and interdental fricatives,

47

in Spanish the distinction is allophonic whereas in English it is phonemic. That is, the difference is meaningful in English but not in Spanish. Because the sounds are not new or difficult to learn little practice should be required to attain mastery of this part of Spanish phonology.

FONEMA /s/

   Cinco alófonos
   [s], [z], [z],
   ̪   •   ̬
   [z], [s]
        ̬

[s]   basta, vista,
 ̪   dentista

Dental, fricativa, oral, sordo. Occurs before /t/.

[z]   posdata, desde,
 •   es difícil

Interdental, fricativa, oral, sonoro. Occurs before /d/.

[z]   Israel, los ríos

Alveolar, fricativa, oral, sonoro. Occurs before /r/.

[z]   mismo, asno,
        periodismo

Dentoalveolar, fricativa, oral, sonoro. Occurs before all other voiced consonants.

[s]   salsas, esposas,
        casa

Dentoalveolar, fricativa, oral, sordo.

PHONEME /s/

   One allophone [s]

[s]   sewn, facing, price

Voiceless, alveolar fricative.

PHONEME /z/

   One allophone [z]

[z]   zone, fazing, prize

Voiced, alveolar fricative

PHONEME /š/

   One allophone [š],
   sometimes written [ʃ]

[š]   sugar, bushel, push

Voiceless, palatal fricative.

PHONEME /ž/

   One allophone [ž],
   sometimes written [ʒ]

[ž] pleasure, rouge

Voiced, palatal fricative.

Does not occur initially.

48

Occurs in all other
positions.

In English the slit fricatives get their
name from the horizontal slit through which the
air is forced to pass (examples, /f/, /v/, /θ/,
/ð/). The groove fricatives are named from the
fact that they are produced with the tongue
forming a groove in which the outer edges are
tense while the air passes along a trough or
groove towards the lips (examples, /s/, /z/,
/š/, /ž/).

In Spanish, the problem involved in producing the correct allophone of the /s/ hinges
upon one's recognition of the importance and
frequency with which the process of <u>regressive
assimilation</u> (asimilación regresiva) comes into
play. By REGRESSIVE ASSIMILATION is meant that
in a consonant cluster (a group of two or more
consonants), the second consonant influences
the first, affecting the element of voice or
the point of articulation. While little misunderstanding will result from a failure to
articulate these allophones carefully, it will
contribute to a heavy foreign accent if one
doesn't use them correctly.

An exercise such as the following may be
used to help one gain competence in distinguishing
the voiced and voiceless allophones of the Spanish
/s/:

<u>Sordo</u>	<u>Sonoro</u>
mis penas [s]	mis venas [z]
sus patas [s]	sus batas [z]
tres corros [s]	tres gorros [z]
es tensa [s]	es densa [z]

Spanish contrasts with English by its lack
of palatal fricatives, /š/ and /ž/ in most dialects
except that of the Río de la Plata region of
South America and in some variants of the dialect
of Southwest Spanish in the United States.

49

FONEMA /x/

Un alófono [x]

[x]   jota, eje,
      reloj, página

<u>Velar, fricativa,</u>
<u>oral, sordo.</u>

The Spanish phoneme /x/ represents a new
sound for most English-speaking students, and is
articulated in the same place as the fricative
[g], with the dorsum of the tongue almost touching
the velum. It may not be substituted by an
English /h/ without causing a heavy accent.

CONTINUANTS

The next class of consonants we shall
discuss are the <u>continuants</u> (continuas), a mis-
celaneous grouping of sounds which generally
obstruct the air passage less than do the stops
and the fricatives. In some systems the continuants are a sub-class of the fricatives.

CONTINUAS	CONTINUANTS
/y/, /w/	/y/, /w/, /h/
FONEMA /y/	PHONEME /y/
Dos alófonos [y], [ǰ]	One allophone [y]
[ǰ] el yeso, el yanqui deshielo, abyecto	[y] yoke, few, onion
<u>Palatal, africado,</u> <u>oral, sonoro.</u>	<u>Voiced, palatal continuant</u> (or <u>semiconsonant</u>).
Occurs after a nasal, a lateral, or a voiced fricative, and in free variation	Forms the first half of many diphthongs.

50

when beginning an accented syllable. By _affricate_ (africado) is meant a compound sound made up of a stop and a fricative.

PHONEME /h/

One allophone [h]

[h] hip, unhappy

Voiceless, glottal (or _pharyngeal) continuant._ Sometimes also called a _spirant._ Linguists do not all agree on the place of articulation. Our preference is to call it glottal.

Alófono [y̆]

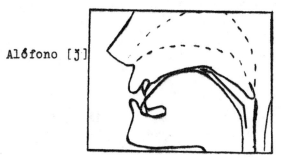

[y] yo, ya, apoyo, hielo

Palatal, continua o _semiconsonante, oral, sonoro._ Many linguists distinguish between the [y] as a consonant and the [j] as a semi-consonant. They also label the [y] a fricative instead of a continuant.

Occurs in all other positions

It is helpful once again to practice distinguishing the two allophones of the Spanish /y/ through a contrastive exercise like this:

Continua [y]	Africado [ǰ]
hielo	con hielo
hierba	con hierba
yunque	el yunque
yermo	un yermo
yerbas	las yerbas

In our system of transcription, both the Spanish and the English /y/'s are used as semiconsonants in forming diphthongs. By SEMICONSONANT (semiconsonante) is meant that the sound has aspects of both a consonant and a vowel, but that it resembles a consonant slightly more. In the two languages, like the other semiconsonant /w/, it forms the first half of those diphthongs which end in vowels. When we reach the discussion of vowels, we will complete this discussion by showing all the possible semiconsonants and semivowels for Spanish with examples of each.

Note here that Spanish [ǰ] is an allophone of the phoneme /y/, and that it therefore does not contrast phonemically with it as in English.

FONEMA /w/

Dos alófonos
[w̌], [w]

[w̌] un hueso, él huele
sin huelga

In many dialects of Spanish this allophone occurs as the first part of a diphthong following a nasal or lateral and in free

PHONEME /w/

One allophone [w]

[w] we, tower, lower

Voiced, bilabial continuant (or semiconsonant).

52

variation when be-
ginning a stressed
syllable. It is a
co-articulated semi-
consonant, by which we
mean that two sounds
are produced simul-
taneously—in this
case both a [w] and
a [g].

Bilabial, continua
o semiconsonante,
oral, sonoro.
        +
Velar, fricativa,
oral, sonoro.

[w]   bueno, antiguo,
      huesudo

Bilabial, continua
o semiconsonante,
oral, sonoro.

It is the first part
of the diphthong which
may occur in all other
positions.

AFFRICATES

The next class of consonants which we shall
discuss are the affricates. By AFFRICATE (africado) is meant a compound consonant sound that
is formed by a brief stoppage of the air stream
followed by a fricative release. To say it
another way, it is the combination of a stop and
a fricative.

AFRICADO   AFFRICATES

/č/   /č/, /ǰ/

53

FONEMA /č/

    Un alófono [č]

[č] china, nacho leche

Palatal, africado, oral, sordo.

PHONEME /č/ sometimes written /tš/ or /tʃ/.

One allophone [č]

[č] churches, etch, chin

Voiceless, alveo-palatal, affricate.

PHONEME /ǰ/ sometimes written /dž/ or /dʒ/.

One allophone [ǰ]

[ǰ] judges, edge, gin

Voiced alveo-palatal, affricate.

    Spanish and English /č/ are very similar, with the main difference being that in the SPANISH /č/, the tip of the tongue usually touches the lower teeth so that the sound is made entirely with the blade and center of the tongue (see the diagram for the articulation of the alófono [ǰ], p. 51). When producing the ENGLISH /č/ and /ǰ/, however, the tip of the tongue normally starts by touching the alveolar ridge and then shifts so that the blade finishes the sound as in Spanish. Substitution of the English sound for the Spanish /č/ causes only a light accent.

LATERALS

    The next group of consonant sounds which we shall describe is that of the laterals. By LATERAL (lateral) we mean that the consonant is a kind of sound which allows the air stream to escape from the mouth by flowing past both sides of the tongue (which is touching the roof of the mouth at one of several possible places).

LATERALES

/l/, /l̯/

LATERAL

/l/

54

FONEMA /l/

    Cuatro alófonos
    [l], [l̪], [l̺],[l̂]

[l̺] saldo, falta,
    suelto

Dental, lateral, oral,
sonoro.

Occurs before a dental.
————————————————
[l̪] alrededor,
    el río

Alveolar, lateral,
oral, sonoro.

Occurs before an
alveolar.
————————————————
[l̂] pelcha, Melchor,
    el yunque

Palatal, lateral,
oral, sonoro.

Occurs before a palatal.
————————————————
[l] Lola, leal

Dentoalveolar, lateral,
oral, sonoro.

Occurs in all other
positions.
————————————————
FONEMA /l̂/ (España)

    Un alófono [l̂]

[l̂] llama, ella,
    calle

PHONEME /l/

    Three principal allo-
    phones [L̥], [l̪], [L̺]

[L̥] play, clay

Voiceless, alveolar
lateral.

In rapid speech, it occurs
after a voiceless stop.
The circle under the
symbol ̥ indicates an
alveolar sound.
————————————————
[l̪] long, fallen, tall

Voiced, alveolar lateral.

Occurs in all other posi-
tions.
————————————————
[L̺] bottle, uncle, bubble

Voiced, alveolar lateral.
The "syllabic-l".

In free variation, this
symbol may be used to
transcribe the /l/
following a stop when it
forms an unstressed
syllable in itself—
usually immediately following a stressed syllable.
In bottle, for example, it
is normally pronounced
[bárl̺]. In careful ar-
ticulation or slow speech
some individuals pronounce
it [bátəl].

55

<u>Palatal</u>, <u>lateral</u>, <u>oral</u>,
<u>sonoro</u>.

This sound, represented
graphically by <u>ll</u>, is
a compound sound
consisting of a
lateral followed by
a palatal. In
Spanish America,
this grapheme is pro-
nounced as the
phoneme /y/ except
in Colombia where it
retains the phonemic
/l/, and Argentina where
it becomes /ž/.

The difference between English /l/ and
Spanish /l/ is two-fold. In the first place,
English /l/ is usually alveolar, whereas Spanish
/l/ is most often dento-alveolar or dental.
Even more noticeable is that when making an
English /l/, speakers have the tendency to hollow
the tongue so that a fairly large cavity is
created between the tongue and the roof of the
mouth. This tendency is especially exaggerated
in the articulation of the "syllabic-l". When
articulating the Spanish /l/, on the other hand,
there is normally much less space between the
tongue and the roof of the mouth. Failure to
reproduce these qualities in either language will
constitute a fairly heavy accent, but will
usually not cause misunderstanding.

NASALS

The NASALS (nasales) are those continuants
which are produced in such a way as to allow the
air to flow through the nasal cavity while at
the same time preventing it from escaping from
the mouth by impeding it at some point. (A
nasal vowel may be produced by allowing the air
to escape from both the mouth and the nose.)

NASALES	NASALS
/m/, /n/, /ñ/	/m/, /n/, /ŋ/

FONEMA /m/ — PHONEME /m/

NASALES — Spanish column:

Dos alófonos
[ɱ], [m]

[ɱ] confianza, sin fin

Labiodental, continua,
nasal, sonoro.

Occurs before /f/.

---

[m] mima, invierno,
momia

Bilabial, continua,
nasal, sonoro.

NASALS — English column:

One allophone [m]

[m] more, summer, sum

Voiced, bilabial nasal.

FONEMA /n/ — PHONEME /n/

Spanish column:

Cinco alófonos
[n], [n̪], [ň],

[ŋ], [n]

[n] (España)

[n̪] dental, santo,
andar

Dental, continua,
nasal, sonoro.

Occurs before a dental.

---

[n] (en España)
onza, sencillo

Interdental, continua,
nasal, sonoro.

English column:

Two allophones
[n], [N]

[n] nor, sinner, sun

Voiced, alveolar nasal.

[N] button, cotton

Voiced, alveolar nasal.

The "syllabic-n" which
occurs as the final
syllable in rapid speech
following a stressed
syllable ending in a
voiceless stop.

In Spain, it occurs
before an interdental.
(/θ/).

[ṇ] Enrique, honrar,
      en Roma

Alveolar, continua,
nasal, sonoro.

[ň] Pancho, poncho
      sin yegua

Alveopalatal, continua,
nasal, sonoro.

Occurs before palatals.

[ŋ] tengo, ancla,
      cinco, estanque   PHONEME /ŋ/

Velar, continua,   One allophone [ŋ]
nasal, sonoro.
                                [ŋ] singer, sung, rung
Occurs before a velar,   Voiced, velar nasal.
and in free variation
before a pause.

---

[n] nombran, banana,
      sino

Dentoalveolar,
continua, nasal,
sonoro.

Occurs in all other
positions.

FONEMA /ñ/

      Un alófono [ñ]

[ñ] ñapa, niño, cañón

Palatal, continua,

58

nasal, sonoro.

Spanish and English /m/ are identical. The major allophone of the Spanish /n/ is dentoalveolar while English /n/ is alveolar, but production of one in place of the other causes only a slight accent, and seldom results in failure to communicate. It should be noted however that because of regressive assimilation, the Spanish /n/ tends to have more allophones than does the English /n/. Notice also that /ŋ/ is a phoneme in English while [ŋ] is only an allophone in Spanish. The main problem facing the English-speaking student of Spanish is that he or she must learn to regularly anticipate the coming sound—especially important when dealing with the Spanish phonemes /n/, /l/, and /s/.

VIBRANTS and RETROFLEX

The next two sounds we are going to discuss are represented graphically in both languages by the letter r. Because the sounds which they represent are so very different however, linguists use two different terms to describe them. For describing the Spanish sound, a convenient term has been vibrant, of which there are two subclasses: simple and multiple. By VIBRANT (vibrante) we mean that the tongue strikes the alveolar ridge rapidly and lightly, once for simple and twice or more for multiple. Many linguists call the simple vibrant a tap or flap, and the multiple vibrant a trill. In Great Britain the letter r is quite often articulated as a flap or tap, but in the dialect of English that most Americans speak, the /r/ is pronounced as a retroflex. The RETROFLEX, like the American /l/, is produced in such a way as to create a large cavity between the tongue and the roof of the mouth with the tip of the tongue flexing back towards the hard palate (from which we derive the term, retroflex).

VIBRANTES   RETROFLEX

/r/, /r̄/   /r/

FONEMA /r/

    Un alófono [r]

[r] aurora, surgir,
     trece

<u>Alveolar</u>, <u>vibrante
simple</u>, <u>oral</u>, <u>sonoro</u>.

FONEMA /r̄/

    Un alófono [r̄]

[r̄] rey, enriquecer,
     hierro, porra

<u>Alveolar</u>, <u>vibrante
múltiple</u>, <u>oral</u>, <u>sonoro</u>.

PHONEME /r/

    Three allophones
    [Ɍ], [Ṛ], [R]

[Ɍ] try, spry, cry

<u>Voiceless</u>, <u>alveo-palatal
retroflex</u>.

Occurs after a voiceless
stop.

[Ṛ] supper, waiter,
    maker

<u>Voiced</u>, <u>alveo-palatal
(syllabic) retroflex</u>.

As with the [Ḷ], in
unstressed syllables
containing only the
retroflex, the term
"syllabic-r" is appro-
priate. The word <u>spotter</u>
would be transcribed
[spárṚ] in normal speech
and in careful or slow
speech [spátəR]. In
most systems based
solely on English, the
commonly used symbol
is [ṛ].

[R] red, rider, drier

<u>Voiced</u>, <u>alveo-palatal
retroflex</u>.

Occurs in all other posi-
tions.

    In most systems based upon English, the
American English <u>r</u> is symbolized phonetically
by linguists as /r/ and [r]. This is not entirely

feasible for a study emphasizing Spanish. We
all recognize that there is a considerable difference between the Spanish and the American
English interpretation of the letter, and so for
the sake of clarity we have opted to show Spanish
as /r/ and [r], and English as /r/ and [R].
Production of English [R] in Spanish constitutes
one of the most characteristic elements of a
heavy American accent, and may occasionally
lead to a failure to communicate.

REVIEW and EXERCISES

1. With the chart included on the following (p.62)
page in mind, go through the following list of
Spanish words and indicate the appropriate
phonetic symbol in the space provided:

EXAMPLE: [r] lira

1. ___ hablar		21. ___ afgano
2. ___ invierno		22. ___ gozar (España)
3. ___ apuesto		23. ___ juzgar (España)
4. ___ otro		24. ___ prosa
5. ___ hasta		25. ___ caldo
6. ___ acaso		26. ___ asno
7. ___ tengo		27. ___ desde
8. ___ codo		28. ___ ojo
9. ___ cuanto		29. ___ haya
10. ___ puño		30. ___ el yunque
11. ___ cero		31. ___ mucho
12. ___ perro		32. ___ salto
13. ___ salgo		33. ___ malo
14. ___ sufrir		34. ___ alrededor
15. ___ colcha		35. ___ imposible
16. ___ confiar		36. ___ mundo
17. ___ enero		37. ___ Enrique
18. ___ ancho		38. ___ venganza (España)
19. ___ vengo		39. ___ agricultor
20. ___ encías		40. ___ lista

2. To help associate similarities and differences
between the various allophones of Spanish consonants
let us review them by explaining which member of
each of the following groups is not appropriate (p.63)

61

PUNTO DE ARTICULACIÓN

MODO DE ARTICULACIÓN	Bilabial	Labio-dental	Inter-dental	Dental	Dento-alveolar	Alveolar	Palatal	Velar
Oclusivo	p b			t d			c ɟ	k g
Africado							č ǰ	
Fricativa	β	f v	θ ð	ş z	s z	z		x ɣ
Nasal	m	ɱ	ṇ	n	n	ņ	ñ	ŋ
Lateral			ḷ	l	l	ḷ	ḷ	
Vibrante						r ř		
Continua/Semi-consonante	ʍ w						y	

The left half of each box contains the voiceless allophone, and the right the voiced one.

and why.

> EXAMPLE: [p t k g] the [g] because it
>   ,   is voiced—the
>   rest are voiceless.
>   (More than one an-
>   swer is possible
>   for some.)

1. [b d g x] the [ ] because _____
2. [l s n d] the [ ] because _____
3. [k x ŋ n] the [ ] because _____
4. [p f b t] the [ ] because _____
5. [f v ŋ b] the [ ] because _____
6. [b f s t] the [ ] because _____
7. [θ s g x] the [ ] because _____

3. To help review Spanish descriptive terminology
use the Spanish four-point system to describe these sounds:

> EXAMPLE: lago <u>Velar, fricativa, oral,</u>
>   <u>sonoro.</u>

1. peras   _____
2. enfático _____
3. robar   _____
4. verde   _____
5. cinco   _____
6. Now go back to question #1 in this
exercise (p. 61) and describe the sounds
for which you supplied the phonetic symbol.

4. To help review English descriptive terminology
use the English three-point system to describe
these sounds:

> EXAMPLE: lake <u>Voiceless velar stop.</u>

1. pears   _____
2. emphatic _____
3. robber   _____

4. verdant _____
5. measure _____

5. Now the languages will be mixed in the same
type of exercise. The purpose is to help under-
line some of the principles of English-Spanish
contrastive analysis. Describe the indicated
sounds using the three-point system for English
and the four-point system for Spanish:

1. laugh   [ ] _____
2. carcajada [ ] _____
3. river   [ ] _____
4. ribera   [ ] _____
5. log   [ ] _____
6. lago   [ ] _____
7. jamón   [ ] _____
8. jam   [ ] _____
9. ingerir   [ ] _____
10. engineer [ ] _____
11. pintar   [ ] _____
12. paint   [ ] _____
13. placer   [ ] _____
14. pleasure [ ] _____
15. enriquecer[ ] _____

6. To review the material in yet another way,
in the following exercise the linguistic description will be provided. Supply the appropriate
phonetic symbol at the left, and a word with an
example of the appropriate sound to the right:

EXAMPLE: [x] Velar, fricativa, oral, sordo
                                      lejos

1. [ ] Bilabial, fricativa, oral, sonoro ___
2. [ ] Voiceless, palatal fricative _____
3. [ ] Velar, fricativa, oral, sonoro _____
4. [ ] Voiced, alveolar stop _____
5. [ ] Dentoalveolar, fricativa, oral, sordo

6. [ ] Voiced, palatal fricative _____
7. [ ] Dentoalveolar, fricativa, oral,
       sonoro
8. [ ] Voiced, alveo-palatal affricate_____
9. [ ] Palatal, africado, oral, sordo _____

64

10. [ ] Voiced, velar stop _____
11. [ ] Labiodental, continua, nasal, sonoro _____
12. [ ] Voiced, bilabial stop _____
13. [ ] Velar, continua, nasal, sonoro _____
14. [ ] Voiceless, interdental fricative _____

15. [ ] Dental, lateral, oral, sonoro _____
16. [ ] Interdental, fricativa, oral, sordo _____
17. [ ] Voiceless, bilabial stop _____
18. [ ] Alveolar, vibrante simple, oral, sonoro _____
19. [ ] Voiceless, alveolar lateral _____
20. [ ] Dental, continua, nasal, sonoro _____

21. [ ] Voiced, velar nasal _____
22. [ ] Velar, oclusivo, oral, sordo _____
23. [ ] Voiceless, velar stop _____
24. [ ] Alveolar, vibrante múltiple, oral, sonoro _____
25. [ ] Voiceless, labiodental fricative _____

7. The final exercise in this section requires
a similar kind of knowledge. Indicate which
language is described by the symbol:

	Español	Inglés
EXAMPLES:		
/č/	sí	sí
/r/	sí	sí
[x]	sí	no
1. /đ/	_____	_____
2. [ǰ]	_____	_____
3. [s]	_____	_____
4. [ẓ]	_____	_____
5. [š]	_____	_____

REVIEW OUTLINE

For review and for future reference, we now
include a chart for Spanish which shows all the

consonant phonemes, the major allophones that we
have discussed, their distribution and an example
of each:

PHONEME	ALLOPHONES	DISTRIBUTION	EXAMPLES
STOPS			
/p/	[p]	All positions	papá
		May not occur word final	propio
/t/	[t̪]	All positions	tonto
			déficit
/k/	[k]	All positions	coloquio
		May not occur word final	kiosco
/b/	[b]	After a pause or nasal	beso, ambos
	[ƀ]	All other positions	hablaba
		May not occur word final	pobre
/d/	[d̪]	After a pause, a nasal or	doy, hundir
		a lateral	falda
	[đ]	All other positions	ardid
/g/	[g]	After a pause or a nasal	gracias
			anglo
	[ǥ]	All other positions	zigzag
FRICATIVES			
/f/	[v]	Before voiced fricative	afgano
	[f]	All other positions	fin, rosbif
/θ/	[z̩]	Before voiced consonant	juzgo
	[θ̩]	All other positions	diez
/s/	[s̪]	Before /t/	basta
	[z̪]	Before /d/	desde
	[ẕ]	Before /r/	Israel
	[z]	Before all other voiced con-	
		sonants	mismo
	[s]	All other positions	salsas
/x/	[x]	All positions	Jauja
AFFRICATE			
/č/	[č]	All positions	chato
		May not occur word final	chicha
LATERALS			
/l/	[l̪]	Before dental (/t/ or /d/)	alta
	[ḷ̩]	Before vibrant /r̄/	alrededor
	[l]	Before palatal /č/ or /y/	colcha
	[l̂]	All other positions	leal

| /l/ | [l] | All positions | llama |
| | | May not occur word final | callar |

VIBRANTS

/r/	[r]	All positions	armario
		May not occur after nasal or pause	
/r̄/	[r̄]	All positions	ropa, perro

CONTINUANTS (including NASALS)

/y/	[ǰ]	After a nasal or lateral	conyugal
		Free variation after pause	
	[y]	All other positions	mayo
/w/	[w]	All positions	huerta
		Must be followed by a vowel, and may not occur word final	
/m/	[ɱ]	Before [f]	enfermo
	[m]	All other positions	mimar
		May not occur word final	
/n/	[n̪]	Before dental (/t/ or /d/)	bandito
	[n̦]	Before vibrant /r̄/	honrar
	[ñ]	Before palatal /č/, /y/, /l/	henchir
	[ŋ]	Before velar, and optional before a pause	rango
	[n̦]	Before interdental /θ/	lince
	[n]	All other positions	nominan
/ñ/	[ñ]	All positions	ñoño
		May not occur word final	

VOWELS

      Having already examined the consonants of Spanish in very great detail, it is appropriate that we complete our discussion of the segmental phonemes of the two languages by comparing and contrasting their vowel phonemes.

      As with the consonants, the vowels may be described by the place in which they are articulated. The traditional manner of showing their articulatory pattern has been to use the device known as the VOWEL TRIANGLE (triángulo de vocales), as in the example at the top of the next page:

67

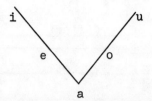

The triangle shows the relative position of articulation inside the mouth. As the diagram suggests, the i and the u are made with the tongue higher in the mouth than with the e, the o or the a. For greater clarity, however, we need to refine it somewhat in order to be able to contrast English and Spanish more effectively.

For that reason let us offer a stylized drawing of the mouth, dividing the oral cavity into nine sections in this way:

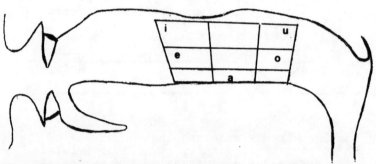

The drawing is especially useful in that it now distinguishes nine separate areas of vowel articulation. These areas are needed in order to describe English vowels adequately. Most traditional descriptions of Spanish vowels have used a much simpler system, limited to two vocales cerradas (/i/ and /u/), one vocal abierta (/a/), and one vocal anterior (/e/) and one vocal posterior (/o/). While this system served for Spanish in the past, it is not really detailed enough to permit a contrasting of Spanish and English. For that

68

reason, let us reproduce the nine-category system with the appropriate locational labels this time, and also include a modified <u>phonemic</u> representation of English and Spanish vowels.

/i/		/u/	High
/I/ /e/ /ɛ/	/ʌ/ /ə/	/ʋ/ /o/	Mid
/æ/	/a/	/ɔ/	Low
Front	Central	Back	

To make these symbols more meaningful, we include a representative list of words containing these vowel sounds. In all cases except the schwa (/ə/), we are discussing stressed vowels (accented vowels).

SPANISH

/i/ p<u>i</u>so, m<u>i</u>ra

/e/ p<u>e</u>so, m<u>e</u>ra

/a/ p<u>a</u>so, m<u>a</u>ra

/o/ p<u>o</u>so, m<u>o</u>ra

/u/ p<u>u</u>so, m<u>u</u>ra

ENGLISH

/i/ b<u>ea</u>t, m<u>ee</u>t [i^i]

/I/ b<u>i</u>t, m<u>i</u>tt

/e/ b<u>ai</u>t, m<u>a</u>te [e^i]

/ɛ/ b<u>e</u>t, m<u>e</u>t

/æ/ b<u>a</u>t, m<u>a</u>t

/a/ p<u>o</u>t, kn<u>o</u>t

/ʌ/ p<u>u</u>tt, m<u>u</u>tt

/ɔ/ b<u>ou</u>ght, t<u>au</u>ght [$ɔ^w$]

/o/ b<u>oa</u>t, m<u>oa</u>t [o^w]

/ʋ/ p<u>u</u>t, f<u>oo</u>t

/u/ b<u>oo</u>t, h<u>oo</u>t [u^w]

69

The modified phonemic vowel system which we have presented here for English has been greatly simplified so as not to show on-glide and off-glide on the left (but one possible phonetic interpretation of the vowel on the right). We recognize that there are very great differences between English and Spanish vowels, and that many of the vowels of English tend to be diphthongized. For that reason we will use both a modified phonemic system (indicated by slashes //) as well as our own variation of the standard allophonic system (indicated by brackets []). In addition, UNSTRESSED English vowels tend to centralize and are usually transcribed phonemically as / /, so that the word, phonology, would be transcribed /fənáləji/, and parliament would be /páRləmənt/.

EXERCISE

For practice in the employment of this system, let us transcribe a few representative Spanish and English words. In addition to applying the vowel transcription system, it will also serve to refresh the system used for the consonants:

SPANISH	ENGLISH
1. hombre [ómbre]	1. man [m æn]
2. informativa [iɱformatíba]	2. infórmative [InfóRmətIv]
3. sububaja _____	3. seesaw _____
4. ferrocarril _____	4. railroad _____
5. carrera _____	5. race _____
6. acera _____	6. sidewalk [sá^{i}dwɔlk]or [wɔk]
7. riquísimo _____	7. delicious _____
8. murciélago _____	8. bat _____

DIPHTHONGS

Both Spanish and English make extensive use of diphthongs, with English employing them more frequently. By DIPHTHONG (diptongo) we mean the combination in a single syllable of a vowel and either a SEMICONSONANT (semiconsonante) or

70

a SEMIVOWEL (semivocal). In Spanish the semi-consonants are [y] and [w], and the semivowels are [i̯] and [u̯]. The semiconsonant precedes the vowel in RISING DIPHTHONGS (diptongos crecientes):

[ye]	siete	[wi]	cuidado
[ya]	farmacia	[we]	suerte
[yo]	odio	[wa]	cuando
[yu]	ciudad	[wo]	cuota

The semivowel follows the vowel in FALLING DIPH-THONGS (diptongos decrecientes):

[ei̯]	seis	[eu̯]	Europa
[ai̯]	baile	[au̯]	jaula
[oi̯]	voy	[ou̯]	bou (trawling)

Both languages also make use of the phe-nomenon known as the TRIPHTHONG (triptongo) which consists of three elements: 1. a semiconsonant followed by 2. a vowel followed by 3. a semivowel. Spanish triphthongs are most commonly used in Spain where the vosotros form of the verb is commonly used. Some examples of Spanish triph-thongs are:

[yei̯]	apreciéis	[wai̯]	apaciguáis
[yai̯]	estudiáis	[wei̯]	buey

REVIEW and EXERCISE

While recognizing that this section has presented both English and Spanish vowels in a greatly simplified manner, the student is now adequately prepared for more advanced studies in segmental phonology. The advanced texts available in phonology are numerous and quite good—phonology is probably the most thoroughly studied aspect of Spanish linguistics.

Let us now try to put everything together that we have learned to this point by transcribing

71

some representative Spanish and English proverbs
(refranes), which are usually poetic, folk-sayings:

1. La zorra mudará los dientes, mas no las mientes.

[la/so/r̄a/mu/da/ra/loz/dyen/tes//maz/no/laz/myen/tes]

> The slashes (/) are used to divide syllables,
> and the double slash (//) indicates a pause
> which is usually represented in writing with
> a comma or a period. Notice the importance
> of regressive assimilation in the phrases,
> los dientes [loz/dyen/tes] and las mientes
> [laz/myen/tes]. The /s/ before a voiced
> consonant becomes voiced, and the nasal
> in both nouns accomodates itself to the
> same point of articulation as the following
> stop.

2. Más sabe el diablo por viejo que por diablo.

[ma/sa/bel/dya/blo/ _____]

> Note that the vowel ending one word joins
> with the vowel beginning the next word;
> sabe + el becomes [sa/bel]. This process
> is usually called SYNALEPHA (sinalefa).
> In addition to vowels, consonants may also
> be linked in the same manner, as in más +
> sabe [ma/sa/be].

3. En boca cerrada no entran moscas.

[em/bo/ka _____ /nᵂoen/tra/mos/ _____

> The /o/ at the end on one word tends to
> velarize and to form a diphthong when the
> word which follows begins with a vowel such
> as /e/. Many different means are used to
> transcribe this example of synalepha, but
> we suggest the compromise shown in the
> example, no + entran as [nᵂoen/tra/mos/].

4. A caballo regalado no hay que mirarle el diente.

---

5. Aunque la mona se vista de seda mona se queda.

6. Dime con quien andas y te diré quien eres.

7. Del dicho al hecho hay gran trecho.

8. Más vale pájaro en mano que cien volando.

9. Aunque son del mismo barro, no es lo mismo bacín que jarro.

10. Ojos que no ven, corazón que no siente.

Now let us try the same thing with a set of English proverbs (using a modified phonetic transcription):

1. You can't make a silk purse out of a sow's ear.

$[yu^W/k^haent/me^ik/ \partial/sIlk/p\Lambda Rs/a^Wt/ \partial v/a/sa^Wz/IR]$
    We have chosen to transcribe the English
off-glides as above to prevent their
being confused with the similar but not
exactly alike Spanish diphthongs. In our
system, the words, <u>out</u>, <u>make</u> and <u>sow's</u> are
transcribed $[a^Wt]$, $[me^ik]$, and $[sa^Wz]$.
The stressed mid-central vowel in English
<u>purse</u> is transcribed as $[\Lambda]$, while the un-
stressed mid-central vowel in the word, <u>of</u>
is transcribed $[\partial]$.

2. Hindsight is better than foresight.

[ha^i nd/sa^i t/Iz/_____

3. The squeaking wheel gets the grease.

[_____

4. For every Jack there's a Jill.

[_____ _____

5. Men make houses but women make homes.

[_____

DISTINCTIVE FEATURES

As the product of the tremendous innovations
brought about by the influence of transformational
grammar, many studies of phonology in English and
in Spanish now utilize a system somewhat different
from the one introduced in this chapter. The
system favored by most transformationalists contains plus and minus features within the general
system known as distinctive features (rasgos
distintivos). What this means is that individual
elements in a complete description of a given
sound are noted with a PLUS (meaning that the
feature is found in the sound being analyzed) or
a MINUS (meaning that the feature is not found).
(Some preparation for using this system is
provided in exercise 2, p. 63 of this chapter.)
While there is considerable discussion among
linguists as to which features are necessary
for an adequate description of the sounds of
Spanish, on the next page you will find a fairly
standard presentation of the major Spanish
allophones. The system provides a very convenient
way to summarize the major elements of the segmental phonemes of Spanish. We see at a glance that
the Spanish [g] for example, is plus: consonantal,
continuant, fricative, voice, labial (when co-
articulated with [w]), high and velar.

74

FEATURE

1. Consonante (Consonantal)
2. Vocal (Vocalic)
3. Nasal (Nasal)
4. Continua (Continuant)
5. Oclusivo (Stop)
6. Africado (Affricate)
7. Fricativa (Fricative)
8. Sonoro (Voice)
9. Labial (Labial)
10. Cerrado (High)
11. Abierto (Low)
12. Velar (Back)

REPRESENTATIVE ALLOPHONES

	1 Consonante	2 Vocal	3 Nasal	4 Continua	5 Oclusivo	6 Africado	7 Fricativa	8 Sonoro	9 Labial	10 Cerrado	11 Abierto	12 Velar
p	+	−	−	−	+	−	−	−	+	−	−	−
t	+	−	−	−	+	−	−	−	−	+	−	−
k	+	−	−	−	+	−	−	−	−	+	−	+
b	+	−	−	−	+	−	−	+	+	−	−	−
β	+	−	−	+	−	−	+	+	+	−	−	−
d	+	−	−	−	+	−	−	+	−	+	−	−
ð	+	−	−	+	−	−	+	+	−	+	−	−
g	+	−	−	−	+	−	−	+	−	+	−	+
ǥ	+	−	−	±+	−	−	+	+	−	+	−	+
f	+	−	−	+	−	−	+	−	+	−	−	−
s	+	−	−	+	−	−	+	−	−	+	−	−
x	+	−	−	+	−	−	+	−	−	+	−	+
θ	+	−	−	+	−	−	+	−	−	−	−	−
z	+	−	−	+	−	−	+	+	−	+	−	−
c	+	−	−	−	+	+±	+	−±	−	+	−	−
ɟ	+	−	−	−	+	+±	+	+±	−	+	−	−
y	+±	±−	−	+	−	−	+±	+	−	+	−	−
l	+	−	−	+	−	−	−	+	−	+	−	−
r	+	−	−	+	−	−	−	+±	−	+	−	−
ř	+	−	−	+	−	−	−	+±	+±	+	−	−
m	+	−	+	−	+	−	−	+	+	−	−	−
n	+	−	+	−	+	−	−	+	−	+	−	−
ñ	+	−	+	−	+	−	−	+	−	+	−	+
i	−	+	−	+	−	−	−	+	−	+	−	−
e	−	+	−	+	−	−	−	+	−	−	−	−
a	−	+	−	+	−	−	−	+	−	−	+	−
o	−	+	−	+	−	−	−	+	−	−	−	+

75

1. Why are the [č] and the [ǰ] plus _and_ minus stop and fricative?

2. What features do these allophones share?
   [k g x u]

3. What features do these allophones share?
   [b d z m]

4. Describe the following sounds by naming their _plus_ features:

   [d]_____
   [f]_____
   [y]_____
   [l]_____
   [m]_____
   [i]_____

SUPRASEGMENTAL PHONEMES and INTONATION

To this point our study of phonology has been dealing only with the segmental phonemes of Spanish. In order to complete our study however, we must also examine the role of _suprasegmental phonemes_ (fonemas suprasegmentales). Some linguists call these phonemes _secondary phonemes_ (fonemas secundarios). The entire field may be called simply _intonation_ (entonación).

Generally included in the study of SUPRA-SEGMENTAL PHONEMES (or INTONATION) are: 1. _Pitch_ (nivel de tono), 2. _Stress_ (acento de intensidad), 3. _Pause_ (pausa) or _Glottal closure_ (golpe de glotis). In the following pages we will examine these features one by one.

1. _PITCH_ (nivel de tono). Like the notes of a musical scale, _pitch_ has to do with the musical level of one's voice during the production of an utterance. We can tell that pitch is phonemic from the following minimal pairs:

76

1. Hablas español.	1. ¿Hablas español?
2. Eres de México.	2. ¿Eres de México?

Although the segmental phonemes are identical in
both utterances, we know that there is a difference
in meaning caused by the musical scale of the voice
in making them. This use of the musical scale is
called <u>pitch</u>, and the fact that it produces meaningful differences between otherwise identical utterances makes it phonemic. The same phenomenon is
also characteristic of English:

1. He's in the apartment.
  1. He's in the apartment?

2. She's pretty.
  2. She's pretty?

Most linguists ascribe three levels of pitch
to Spanish and four to English. In addition, the
difference between levels in Spanish is less than
it is for English. We may compare the two scales
in this graphic manner:

Spanish   English

                    4_____
                    3_____
3_____   2_____
2_____
1_____   1_____

Number 1 indicates a low pitch and number 3 a
high one in Spanish. Comparing the use of pitch
in the two languages, it has been said that
Spanish syllables, like little soldiers, march
equally with very little variation in size and
height. English syllables on the other hand are
like a group of civilians, grown-ups and children,
out for a Sunday stroll. (This simile is also
appropriate in comparing vowel length in the two
languages.)

Using these numbers to indicate pitch, let us note a pair of **normal** declarative sentences in both Spanish and English:

```
2               1 1         2          1 1
Se llama Juan Gómez.↓    Vive en Madrid.↓
```

```
2               31      2              3 1
His name is John Smith.↓  He lives in Chicago.↓
```

The pitch pattern for a normal declarative sentence in Spanish generally follows that of the example (2-1-1), with the voice dropping at the end (indicated by the arrow ↓). If this pattern is produced for an English sentence, it creates an impression of aloofness or of boredom.

A normal declarative sentence in English generally follows the pitch pattern of the example above (2-3-1) with the voice dropping at the end. If this pattern is produced for a Spanish sentence it creates the impression of an exclamation, of enthusiasm. While this is usually only a minor problem, it is further complicated when the exclamation pattern for English is produced in Spanish:

```
2             3 3    2      41   2              41
Are you Jim Johnson?  No, I'm not!  I'm Robert Smith!
```

The use of level 4 in English produces an exclamation, but in Spanish use of this level is not meaningful. The result of English intonation in Spanish is that the English-speaking person often appears to be excited and enthusiastic when he or she is not, and to be merely odd when intending to show exclamation.

A comparable exclamatory pattern in Spanish would be:

```
2                   2 2    2    31      2
¿Se llama Luis Martínez?  ¡No, yo no!  ¡Me llamo José
        31
        García!
```

Producing the English interrogative pattern in
Spanish will generally elicit the desired response,
but the English-speaker who is not aware of
Spanish intonation patterns will often fail to
recognize as a question (expecting a yes or no
answer) an utterance having the pitch pattern
2-2-2.

EXERCISE

With the aid of a native-speaker of Spanish
and/or a native-speaker of English (use yourself
as one of the informants), analyze the pitch of
these sentences using the number system we have
introduced in this section. Do not confuse
pitch with stress (loudness). Pay close attention
to the pitch of the last word in all of the sentences which follow:

1. My friend is from Ohio.

   Mi amigo es de Honduras.

2. Where's the book?

   ¿Dónde está el libro?

3. It was extremely interesting!

   ¡Fue sumamente interesante!

4. Jim? Is it really you?

   ¿Juanito? ¿Eres tú?

5. You're going tomorrow, right?

   Tú vas mañana, ¿no?

STRESS

2. STRESS or ACCENT (acento de intensidad).
By STRESS (acento de intensidad) is meant the
loudness of a syllable. Generally speaking,
in both languages there are four levels of stress:
1. Primary or tonic accent (acento principal) which
is the loudest or strongest; 2. Secondary (secun-
dario) which is the next loudest or strongest;
3. Tertiary (tercero), third in strength or loudness;

4. Unstressed (inacentuado) which includes the
remaining unstressed syllables.

To indicate stress we shall use these
generally accepted diacritical marks:

1. Primary accent   ´
2. Secondary accent   ˋ
3. Tertiary accent   ˆ
4. Unstressed   (no mark at all)

As we did with pitch, we are able to demonstrate
that stress too has phonemic value which may be
noted in the following minimal pairs (cotejos):

Spanish

    éste   esté
    pâra el juégo   ¡Pâra el juégo!
      (for the game) (Stop the game!)
    cánto   cantó

English

    the whîte hóuse the Whíte Hóuse
    mỳ tônîghts   mỳ twó knîghts

In normal Spanish sentences, the accented
syllable of most verbs and most nouns carries
a primary stress:

Lâ lúna brîllába cômo sî fuéra de pláta.

The principal difference between English stress
and Spanish stress is that English puts a primary
stress on the contrasting words of a comparison no
matter what parts of speech they may be, while
Spanish rarely puts a primary stress on prepositions or adjectives. For comparison, note these
examples:

It's nót on TÓP of the táble but rather
    underNÉATH the táble.

Nô está encîma de la MÉsa sino
    debàjo de la MÉsa.

80

Do yòu wánt a róom WÍTH méals or withÓUT méals?

¿Deséa una hàbitación cón coMÍdas o sín coMÍdas?

EXERCISE

Once again with the aid of a native speaker
of Spanish and one of English, compare the following
sentences. This will provide the data necessary
to practice the system we have presented for
analyzing stress:

1. He has a small flat in Madrid.
   Tiene un piso pequeño en Madrid.

2. The President lives in the White House.
   El Presidente vive en la Casa Blanca.

3. My book is blue but yours is green.
   El libro mío es azul pero el tuyo es verde.

4. He's a first-year student but she's a third-year
student.

   El es estudiante del primer año pero ella es

   estudiante del tercer año.

Do the languages put primary stress on the same
number of words? On words of the same grammatical
category (nouns, verbs, prepositions)? Are the
generalizations introduced in this section veri-
fied by your evidence?

PAUSE

3. PAUSE (pausa), BOUNDARY ELEMENT or
GLOTTAL CLOSURE (golpe de glotis). A feature
characteristic of English intonation but not
of Spanish is the pause (pausa), boundary element,
or glottal closure. All three terms describe
what is essentially the same feature. Between
words, most easily heard before words which begin
with a vowel, native speakers of English generally
close the glottis momentarily in order to insure
that each word tends to form a discrete unit.

It may be heard between words in a careful articulation of this grouping of words:

    ant, apple, interest
    open, up, uncle

It is even more apparent in the substandard:

    *a apple
    *a actress

We can demonstrate briefly that the use of
pause is phonemic in English through the following
minimal pairs:

    nitrate   night rate
    bootstrap   boots trap

When one seeks to speak especially clearly
in English, each pause will generally bring a
glottal closure at the beginning of the next word.
This characteristic of English is foreign to Spanish
and will occasionally prevent the student from
linking words in the way normal for Spanish
(synalepha). A speaker of English will make an
artificial distinction between these two phrases
in Spanish:

    un artista   una artista

The persistence of English habits here will not
usually cause serious misunderstanding, but it
will contribute to a foreign accent.

SELECTED BIBLIOGRAPHY

Bull, William E. Spanish for Teachers: Applied
    Linguistics. New York: Ronald, 1965.
Cárdenas, Daniel N. Introducción a una comparación
    fonológica del español y del inglés.
    Washington, D.C.: Center for Applied
    Linguistics, 1960.
Cressey, William W. Spanish Phonology and Mor-
    phology: A Generative View. Washington, D.C.:
    Georgetown UP, 1978.

Dalbor, John B. Spanish Pronunciation: Theory
      and Practice. New York: Holt, Rinehart &
      Winston, 1969.
Harris, James. Spanish Phonology. Cambridge, Mass:
      M.I.T., 1969.
Lázaro Carreter, Fernando. Diccionario de términos
      filológicos. Rpt. Madrid: Gredos, 1971.
Mackay, Ian. Introducing Practical Phonetics. Boston:
      Little, Brown, 1978.
Narváez, Ricardo A. Instruction in Spanish
      Pronunciation. 2 Vols. St. Paul: EMC Corp.
      1970.
Navarro Tomás, Tomás. Manual de pronunciación
      española. Rpt. New York: Hafner, 1957.
Politzer, Robert L., & Charles N. Staubach.
      Teaching Spanish: A Linguistic Orientation.
      Lexington, Mass: Xerox, 1965.
Stockwell, Robert P., & J. Donald Bowen. The
      Sounds of English and Spanish. Chicago:
      U. of Chicago P., 1965.
Terrell, Tracy D., & Maruxa Salgués de Cargill.
      Lingüística aplicada a la enseñanza del
      español a angloparlantes. New York: John
      Wiley & Sons, 1979.

Chapter 3

INTRODUCTION TO SPANISH MORPHOLOGY

INTRODUCTION

In this chapter, no longer focusing on single sounds, we shall expand our investigation to include meaningful portions of words as well as words themselves.

Just as "smallest meaningful unit of sound" is one standard definition of <u>phoneme</u>, the "smallest meaningful unit of speech" is an acceptable definition of MORPHEME (morfema). As a phoneme has smaller units within its family called <u>allophones</u>, so too the individual member units in the family of a morpheme are called ALLOMORPHS (alomorfos). These two concepts may perhaps be explained more clearly through example, and for that reason we have created the following nonsense sentence to illustrate the principal elements of the study of morphology:

<u>Aquellos lotecos no gropaban bien los morotes grosestísimos.</u>

Although many of the words in this sentence are unfamiliar because they don't exist, we recognize immediately that the sentence is a Spanish one. We know that the verb is <u>gropaban</u>, and that it is made up of three elements: the stem <u>grop(ar)</u>, the indicator of the imperfect, -<u>aba</u>, and the indicator of the third-person plural subject, -<u>n</u>. These three elements of the verb are <u>morphemes</u>.

From our knowledge of the verb, we suspect that the subject is <u>lotecos</u>, which consists of the morphemes <u>loteco</u>, and the plural marker, -<u>s</u>. Additional infromation to reinforce our recognition of the plural subject comes from the <u>noun determiner</u> (determinante), <u>aquellos</u>, which also consists of two morphemes, <u>aquel(lo)</u> and -<u>s</u>.

It is called a noun determiner because it is used
to modify nouns, and to distinguish them from other
parts of speech.

We further recognize that the sentence is
a Spanish one because the idea of negation is
conveyed by the word, no, placed before the verb,
and that the adverb bien, closely follows the verb.
The final noun phrase with its determiner los, its
noun morotes, and adjective grosestísimos, also
conforms perfectly to the rules of Spanish grammar.

The information we have gathered from this
observation is morphosyntactic (morfosintáctica)
in that it is derived from both morphology (morfología) and syntax (sintaxis). MORPHOLOGY (morfología) then is the study of morphemes and words (a
single morpheme or a combination of morphemes), and
SYNTAX, the study of the arrangement of all the
elements of speech in a language.

MORPHEMES

Already in this brief introduction to morphology we may recognize the existence of two basic
kinds of morphemes:

1. INDEPENDENT or FREE MORPHEMES (morfema
independiente), which are those that may
exist independently or freely in an utterance. The word no and the word bien are
good examples of independent morphemes.

2. DEPENDENT or BOUND MORPHEMES (morfema
dependiente) are those which may not exist
freely in an utterance while still retaining
their meaning. They must be attached to
another morpheme, and in linguistic analyses
they are indicated graphically with a hyphen
(preceding or following the morpheme) at the
place where they join the other morphemes.
Good examples of bound morphemes from the
model sentence include: -s, the indicator of
plural for aquellos, lotecos, los, morotes and
grosestísimos; -n the indicator of the third-

person-plural as the subject of the verb,
gropaban; -aba, the indicator of tense;
ísimo, the indicator of a superlative.

Within the general concept of morpheme,
the individual variants or allomorphs (alomorfos)
are the family members of a single morpheme and
are found to be in complementary distribution
(just as allophones of phonemes are in complementary distribution).

The most well-known example of a common
morpheme having several allomorphs distributed in
this way is the morpheme which expresses the idea
of plural:

1. One common allomorph of the morpheme
plural is /-s/, as in hombres, chicos,
cafés and chicas. It is normally added to
words which end in unaccented vowels or
which end in an accented é.

2. A second allomorph of plural is /-es/,
as in mujeres, edades, rubíes and motores.
It is added to words which end in a consonant
or in an accented vowel (some exceptions of
the latter are noted below).

3. A third allomorph is -Ø (zero allomorph—
alomorfo cero) in which nothing is added
to form the plural, in words such as
cortaplumas, lunes, martes, Cervantes,
García. These nouns are shown to be plural
not by a change in their form but by a
plural noun determiner—los cortaplumas,
los lunes, los martes, los Cervantes, los
García.

Except for the pluralization of family names (which
are morphologically determined—see below) the
above allomorphs are all phonologically determined
in that their form is determined by specific
sound environments as outlined in the three rules
listed above.

A second set of allomorphs within the

87

morpheme of plural includes those which are morphologically determined. This is a phrase linguists
use to explain the apparent exceptions to the three
major rules listed above. Most of the exceptions
which follow result from historical remnants which
have not yet been changed by analogy (the process
of making words, morphemes or sounds conform to
the basic pattern of the language), or foreign
words which have not yet been so fully assimilated
as to lose their foreign association. Examples
of allomorphs which are morphologically determined
(still relating to the morpheme of plural) include:

4. a small group of words which end in an
accented vowel that do not take /-es/ but
rather /-s/: dominós, mamás, papás and
sofás.

5. The word maravedí has three plural
forms: maravedís, maravedíes, and mara-
vedises.

6. Foreign words which do not conform to the
normal phonological determination include:
lores (from lord), clips, clubs and jeeps.

7. Most compound words pluralize the second
element and conform to the phonological
patterns expressed in rules #1 and #2 above.
Exceptions which are morphologically determined include:

a. Those compounds which pluralize the
first element instead of the second:
hijosdalgo and cualesquiera.

b. Those compounds which pluralize
both elements: ricoshombres.

In this rule, the actual sound used to make
the plural is the normal one for Spanish,
but the choice of the stem to which it is
added is morphologically determined.

We may express the major aspects of
these rules in a formula which might look like

88

this:
$$\{-s\} \quad /-s \approx -es \approx -\emptyset/$$

The braces { } indicate that what is contained
inside is morphemic (here, the morpheme of
<u>plural</u>). To the right is indicated the various
allomorphs, the phonological forms which the
plural might take. The symbol $\approx$ indicates that
the items are in complementary distribution.
The slanted bars //, as noted in the study of
phonology, indicate that the sounds contained
between them are phonemes. This formula then,
translated, states that the <u>morpheme</u> of <u>plural</u>
is a dependent morpheme added to the end of a
word (or base), and which consists of three
allomorphs in complementary distribution.

AFFIXATION

Independent morphemes, commonly called
words, are meaningful both in isolation as well
as in an utterance. Dependent morphemes on the
other hand must be attached to another morpheme
or combination of morphemes in order to convey
meaning. The dependent morphemes in Spanish are
attached either to the front of the <u>base</u> or <u>stem</u>
(la base)—the independent morpheme or combination
of morphemes to which it is attached—or at the
end of it. If it is attached to the front it is
called a PREFIX (prefijo), and if it is attached
to the back it is called a SUFFIX (sufijo).
Spanish does not make extensive use of the linguistic phenomenon of the INFIX (infijo) although
some linguists see infixes in the plural <u>-es</u> of
<u>cualesquiera</u>, the <u>-s</u> of <u>hijosdalgo</u>, and the <u>-ar-</u>
of <u>polvareda</u>. The general term, <u>AFFIX</u> (afijo)
may be applied to all three types, and the process of adding an affix to a stem is called
AFFIXATION (afijación).

A variant of this process which occurs
with some frequency in Spanish is called SIMUL-
TANEOUS AFFIXATION (parasíntesis), in which a
prefix and a suffix are added at the same time.
In the word, <u>enriquecer</u>, the prefix <u>en-</u> and the

<u>inchoative</u> <u>suffix</u> (sufijo incoativo) <u>-ecer</u> are
added simultaneously. <u>Inchoative</u> means that the
morpheme denotes the beginning of a state or
condition, and appropriately the meaning of the
verb <u>enriquecer</u> is "to become rich." Other
examples of the same type include: <u>enniñecer</u>,
<u>encarecer</u> and <u>endurecer</u>. Four other types of
simultaneous affixation are also common:

a- + -ar	asustar, agrupar, alargar
en- + -ar	ensillar, enlatar
em- + -ar	embotellar
em- + -ecer	embellecer, embravecer, embrutecer

In the bottom two examples, the prefix <u>en-</u> is
replaced by <u>em-</u>, the allomorph which is phonologically conditioned to occur before a bilabial
(/b/ or /p/).

INFLECTION and DERIVATION

The process of adding affixes, <u>affixation</u>,
may be divided into two general categories:

1. INFLECTION (inflexión). In this process
the addition of an affix does not change the
form class (verb, noun, adjective) of the
stem or change the basic meaning of it. The
change brought about in creating <u>hombres</u>
from <u>hombre</u> (the addition of the plural
morpheme /<u>-s</u>/) is an example of inflection.
The inflected form, <u>hombres</u>, still pertains
to the form class of nouns, and has not
been changed in the intrinsic meaning of
the word—it has simply been multiplied.

2. DERIVATION (derivación). In this
process non-inflectional affixes are added
to the base form in order to create new
words. An example is seen in the difference
between <u>hombre</u> and <u>hombrón</u>. Although in this
case the form class has not been changed,
(both are nouns) the basic meaning of the
stem has been changed considerably, from

90

"man" to "big man". The augmentative
suffix -ón, then, is derivational.

These two terms, inflection and derivation, will
be important to us in this chapter because all the
affixes we shall discuss will be listed in one
category or the other.

INFLECTIONAL SUFFIXES

In Spanish, all inflectional affixes are
suffixes, with the possible exception of those
examples of the morpheme plural which some linguists analyze as infixes (the words cualesquiera
and hijosdalgo). The major inflectional suffixes
for Spanish include:

1. Nouns (nombre or sustantivo). The only
inflectional suffix which may be added to
nouns in Spanish is that of number (making
it singular or plural). The difference
between mujer and mujeres is that of number.
There is some discussion as to whether
gender should be considered an inflectional
suffix for nouns. The consensus seems to
be that gender is not inflectional in nouns,
and that doctor and doctora for example are
not inflectional variants but rather, separate nouns.

2. Adjectives (adjetivo). In addition to
inflection for number, as in verde, verdes,
adjectives in Spanish may also be inflected
to show gender (género) as in rico and rica.

3. Pronouns (pronombre). Pronouns may be
inflected to show number, as in ella, ellas;
to show gender, ellos, ellas; to show
grammatical case (caso gramatical), yo, me,
mí; and to show person (persona) as with
yo, tú, él. Because of their complex history
the forms of the inflections of the pronouns
are virtually all morphologically determined.
(In other words, the inflectional variants
do not fit a perfectly regular pattern.)

91

4. <u>Verbs</u> (verbo). Verbs may be inflected
to show <u>number</u>, as <u>hablo</u>, <u>hablamos</u>; to
show <u>person</u>, as in <u>hablo</u>, <u>hablas</u>; to show
<u>tense</u> (tiempo), as in <u>hablo</u> <u>hablaré</u>; to
show <u>mood</u> (modo), as <u>hablo</u>, <u>hable</u>; and to
show <u>grammatical function</u>, as in <u>hablando</u>,
<u>hablar</u> and <u>hablado</u>.

In the morphological analysis of Spanish
verbs, it may be demonstrated that all verb forms
contain either two or three morphemes which
occur in this sequence:

a. First comes the base or stem, <u>habl-</u>
(the stem of <u>hablar</u>), <u>com-</u> (<u>comer</u>), and
<u>escrib-</u> (<u>escribir</u>). As the dashes suggest,
these stems are dependent morphemes—they
may not exist independently and still retain
their meaning.

b. To the base is added a morpheme showing
tense, mood or grammatical function, such
as <u>-aba</u> to form <u>hablaba</u>, <u>-ar</u> to form <u>hablar</u>,
<u>-ido</u> to form <u>comido</u>, or <u>-iendo</u> to form
<u>comiendo</u>.

c. To the combination of base and tense may
be added a final morpheme of person and
number which usually has the form <u>-s</u>, <u>-mos</u>,
<u>-is</u>, <u>-n</u>, or ∅. The <u>zero</u> (∅) means that the
morpheme does not physically occupy the
slot normally allocated for the morpheme
of person.

While the apparent symmetry of the Spanish verb
system has been inferred, it will become even
more clear in the chart introduced on the next
page (p. 93).

All regular verbs, as we note on the chart,
consist of three dependent morphemes: stem,
tense/mood marker, and person.

STEM	1	2	3	4	5	6	7	PERSON	
habl—	-o	-ába	-é	-aré	-aría	-e	-ára	-Ø	1
	-a	-ába	-á-	-ará	-aría	-e	-ára	-s(te)	2
	-a	-ába	-ó	-ará	-aría	-e	-ára	-Ø	3
	-á	-ába	-á-	-aré	-aría	-é	-ára	-mos	1
	-á	-ába	-áste	-aré	-aría	-é	-ára	-is	2
	-a	-ába	-áro-	-ará	-aría	-e	-ára	-n	3
com—	-o	-ía	-í	-eré	-ería	-a	-iéra	-Ø	1
	-e	-ía	-í-	-erá	-ería	-a	-iéra	-s	2
	-e	-ía	-ió	-erá	-ería	-a	-iéra	-Ø	3
	-é	-ía	-í-	-eré	-ería	-á	-iéra	-mos	1
	-é	-ía	-iste	-eré	-ería	-á	-iéra	-is	2
	-e	-ía	-iéro	-erá	-ería	-a	-iéra	-n	3
abr—	-o	-ía	-í	-iré	-iría	-a	-iéra	-Ø	1
	-e	-ía	-í-	-irá	-iría	-a	-iéra	-s	2
	-e	-ía	-ió	-irá	-iría	-a	-iéra	-Ø	3
	-í	-ía	-í-	-iré	-iría	-á	-iéra	-mos	1
	*í	-ía	-íste	-iré	-iría	-á	-iéra	-is	2
	-e	-ía	-iéro	-irá	-iría	-a	-iéra	-n	3

The numbers at the <u>top</u> indicate tense and mood:
    <u>Tense</u>: 1. present, 2. imperfect, 3. preterit,
        4. future, 5. conditional.
    <u>Mood</u>: 6. present subjunctive, 7. imperfect
        subjunctive.
The numbers at the right indicate person.

*The -í- of the tense/mood morpheme combines with
the -is of the person morpheme to form -ís, in
abrís.

We are now able to make some additional useful
generalizations about Spanish verbs:

    1. The morpheme of <u>person</u> clearly makes a
    distinction between singular and plural
    subjects, and marks all plurals separately.

2. All tense/mood morphemes are distinct from all others except for possible confusion between the first-person plural present and preterit.

3. Because of potential confusion as well in the first and third person singular of the person morpheme, the tense/mood morpheme resolves it in the present indicative, the preterit and the future. Ambiguity and possible confusion remain only for the imperfect, the conditional and the subjunctives.

> This general lack of ambiguity allows Spanish to use the subject pronouns (yo, nosotros, tú, etc.) only for cases of emphasis or for extra clarification. In French and English this is not possible.

4. The tense/mood morpheme also contains verb-class information which is used to distinguish -ar from -er and -ir verbs in all tenses and moods.

5. The Spanish future and conditional are late historical developments, deriving from the habit in the late Middle Ages of conveying the future by using an infinitive plus an appropriate form of haber. "I shall eat" was conveyed in Spanish by the infinitive comer plus he. Comeré was then written as comer he, and comería was comer hía. Because these tenses have been formed from a combination of two words, they are sometimes called periphrastic (perifrástico), meaning that they make use of a helping word.

EXERCISE

To provide for an application of all the information presented to this point, let us once again look at the nonsense sentence which introduced the chapter:

<u>Aquellos lotecos no gropaban bien los morotes</u>
<u>grosestísimos.</u>

1. Starting with the verb, <u>gropaban</u>:

How many morphemes does it contain?
What are their forms? <u>grop</u>- -<u>aba</u>- -<u>n</u>.
What is the meaning of each morpheme?
        grop- (nonsense stem) ‗‗‗‗‗‗‗ ‗‗‗‗‗‗‗
Are the affixes derivational or inflectional?
Dependent or independent?

2. Concerning the subject, <u>lotecos</u>:

How many morphemes does it contain?
What are their forms?
Are the affixes derivational or inflectional?
Bound or free?

3. The final adjective, <u>grosestísimos</u>:

How many morphemes does it contain?
What are their forms?
What are the approximate meanings?
Are they derivational, inflectional, bound
        or free?

Now let us take a real sentence and analyze it
in the same manner:

<u>Los muchachitos aprendieron rápidamente las</u>
<u>lecciones.</u>

1. The verb, <u>aprendieron</u>:

How many morphemes?
What are their forms and meanings?
Are the affixes derivational, inflectional,
        bound, free?

2. The subject, <u>muchachitos</u>:

How many morphemes does it contain?
What are their forms and meanings?

95

What kinds of affixes are they?

3. The determiner, los:

    How many morphemes does it contain?
    What are their forms and approximate mean-
        ings?
    Are they derivational, inflectional,
        bound, free?

4. The adverb, rápidamente:

    How many morphemes does it contain?
    What are their forms and meanings?
    Are they derivational, inflectional,
        bound, free?

IRREGULAR VERBS

    Before moving to a discussion of deriva-
tional affixes, let us pause briefly to consider
two patterns of verb irregularities. For the
most part these irregularities conform to regular patterns of historical sound change phenomena (which will be examined in detail in chapter
5).

    There are a number of verbs with an o in
in the stem which show irregularities in the
present indicative and the present subjunctive,
as does the verb, volver (we use a written
accent on the stressed syllable for greater
clarity):

vuélvo vuélves vuélve vuélven

volvémos volvéis

The reason for these irregularities in the
singular and the third person plural is found
in the historical development from Latin to
Spanish. In a stressed (accented) syllable,
short-o in Latin became open-o in Vulgar Latin
which in turn became the diphthong ue in Spanish.
In vuelvo, for example, the stressed syllable

96

has diphthongized to ue, whereas in volvemos, the o has remained in modern times because it is not part of the stressed syllable. Among the many verbs which follow this pattern of irregularities may be included: acordar, acostar, almorzar, colgar, contar, dormir, morder, morir, mostrar, poder, recordar, rodar, rogar, soler, volcar, volver, etc.

A second common pattern of irregularities, verbs having an e in the stem and an ie in the three forms of the singular and third-person plural of the present indicative and subjunctive, is of similar historical origin. In a stressed syllable, short-e of Latin became open-e in Vulgar Latin and then diphthongized to ie in Spanish. This pattern is seen in the verb, perder (again, we have marked the stressed syllables for the sake of clarity):

piérdo piérdes piérde piérden

perdémos perdéis

In pierdo, the diphthong is the stressed syllable, whereas in perdemos the stress falls on the morpheme of tense which never diphthongized. Verbs which conform to this pattern of irregularities include: acertar, advertir, cegar, cerrar, comenzar, discernir, empezar, entender, negar, perder, querer, sentar, sentir, etc.

DERIVATIONAL AFFIXES

In the section which follows we are going to present a fairly large number of derivational affixes (both prefixes and suffixes) in order to convey a small portion of the immense wealth of morphological resources available to a Spanish-speaking person. By DERIVATION, once again, we mean the process of adding an affix which either changes the form class of the word (from a verb to a noun, for example), or which changes the central meaning of the base or stem, as hombre is changed in meaning when it is converted

97

into hombrón.

We are now ready to offer an extensive listing of derivational suffixes and their meanings. The two primary rules for adding any derivational suffix to a stem are:

1. When a stem ends in an unstressed vowel, this vowel disappears when the suffix is added: niño, niñito; mona, monita.

2. To a base ending in a consonant, the suffix is attached without any change in the base: mujer, mujercita; animal, animalito.

There are other situations which require additional modification of these rules, and which would make our study more complicated at this point than is necessary. For that reason they are not included here. A complete and detailed listing of these rules may be found in Ricardo A. Narváez's An Outline of Spanish Morphology (see bibliography).

A large group of suffixes in Spanish are used to indicate nationality and geographical association and origin. These suffixes are called gentilicios in Spanish, and the most important include:

-aco/a	polaco, polaca
-án/-ana	alemán, alemana
-ano/a	mexicano, mexicana
-ayo/a	uruguayo, uruguaya
-ego/a	gallego, gallega
-eno/a	chileno, chilena
-ense	costarricense (also costarriqueño)
-eño/a	madrileño, madrileña
-eo/a	hebreo, hebrea
-ero/a	habanero, habanera
-és/-esa	holandés, holandesa
-í	israelí
-ino/a	numantino, numantina
-teco/a	guatemalteco, guatemalteca
-tano/a	napolitano, napolitana

There are five important groups of suffixes

which result in nouns (<u>sustantivos</u>). To enhance
the learning experience in this section, fill
in the base word at the right.

1. <u>Collectives</u> (colectivo):

-ada	manada (flock, handful)	mano
-aje	ropaje (clothes)	ropa
-al	dineral, peral	dinero, pera
-ar	pinar, manzanar	
-eda	alameda	
-edo	robledo	

2. <u>Profession</u> or <u>occupation</u> (profesión,
oficio):

-ero/a	zapatero, lavandera	
-ia	boticaria	
-ista	dentista	
-logo	psicólogo, farmacólogo	

3. A <u>blow</u> (golpe):

-ada	pedrada (blow from stone)	
-azo	puñetazo, sablazo	

4. <u>Quality</u>, <u>effect</u> (cualidad):

-ancia	abundancia	abundar
-anza	holganza	
-encia	presidencia	
-dad	dualidad	
-tad	libertad	
-ez	sencillez	
-eza	pereza	
-ia	gracia	
-ie	barbarie	
-tud	plenitud	
-umbre	dulcedumbre, mansedumbre	
-ura	blandura	

5. <u>Action</u> (acción):

-ada	bajada	bajar
-ata	caminata	

99

```
-aje      pillaje              _____
-azo      cañonazo, vistazo    _____
-eo       bloqueo              _____
-ería     cacería              _____
-ura      montura, censura     _____
```

Another group of derivational suffixes is used to form verbs. There are only nine of these verbal suffixes which are productive, however, and most of them are first conjugation verbs ending in -ar.

```
-ear      flirtear, gatear, parquear (to
          perform an action, used especially
          with English loan words.) flirt, gato
-ificar   pacificar            _____
-itar     dormitar (to do in part) _____
-izar     quijotizar           _____
-uar      efectuar             _____
```

The four remaining verbal suffixes tend to be used in simultaneous affixation, in which a prefix and suffix are added at the same time. As with the previous examples (pp. 89-90), these generally relate to the beginning of a state or action:

```
-ecer     entristecer  (en- + -ecer)_____
-entar    emparentar   (em- + -ar)_____
-iar      abreviar     (a-  + -entar)_____
-iguar    apaciguar    (a-  + -iguar)_____
```

EXERCISE

To consolidate this portion of our study of morphology, let us practice using some of the derivational suffixes we have listed:

1. Using gentilicios, we know that a man from Mexico is mexicano.

What is a man who is from Guatemala?_____
Honduras? _____
la Mancha?_____
Paraguay _____

100

Valencia _____
Francia _____
Cuba _____
Puerto Rico _____
Texas _____

2. Because of the large number of Latinate
words in English, a good number of Spanish
suffixes find cognate suffixes in English.
For that reason, the following exercise
in showing the Spanish equivalents should
be an easy one:

carpenter	carpintero	-er	= -ero
circumstance	_____	-ance	= _____
multitude	_____	-tude	= _____
spoonful	_____	-ful	= _____
civilize	_____	-ize	= _____
fortify	_____	-ify	= _____
society	_____	-ty	= _____
ceremony	_____	-mony	= _____

3. As a general review of derivational
suffixes, determine the probable meaning
for these words:

santanderino _____ (What two mor-
              phemes?) _____
puñalada _____ _____
hospedaje _____ _____
naranjal _____ _____
venganza _____ _____
palomar _____ _____
flechazo _____ _____

4. In this exercise, give the meaning of
the derivational suffix and then create
an example word in the space at the right.

-ecer inchoative (beginning) envilecer
-ano _____ _____
-ero _____ _____
-ada _____ _____
-ista _____ _____
-ense _____ _____

101

SUFFIXES OF ATTITUDE

There remain yet four important classes of modificational, derivational suffixes which provide the Spanish-speaking person with the opportunity to express his or her attitude toward the object, idea or person being referred to. Used primarily in conversation, the four modifications are:

1. Augmentative (aumentativo). These suffixes make the described object larger, and frequently convey a negative secondary meaning as well. An equivalent idea is sometimes conveyed in English with the phrase, "big ol'," as in "the big ol' man."

-acho	ricacho	<u>rico</u>
-arrón	chicarrón	
-azo	muchachazo, jefazo	
-etón	mocetón, pobretón	
-ón	hombrón, muchachón	
-ote	coloradote, muchachote	

2. Diminutive (diminutivo). These suffixes make the object described seem smaller, and they frequently convey an affectionate, appreciative attitude. An equivalent idea is sometimes conveyed in English with the word, "little" and the suffix -ie or -y, [i], as in, "my little sweety."

-ito	animalito	<u>animal</u>
-illo	geniecillo, golfillo	
-ico	gatico	
-uelo	riachuelo, rapazuelo (urchin)	
-ín	pajarín, pequeñín	
-ino	colino	<u>col</u>
-ejo	animalejo	
-ete	vejete	
-ón	usually augmentative, it is diminutive in these three examples: ratón, callejón, cerrejón	

3. **Appreciative** (apreciativo). These suffixes convey an attitude that favorably disposes the listener to the word. This idea is sometimes conveyed in English with the phrase, "good ol'," as in "the good ol' boys," or "sweet little" as in "that sweet little thing." In Spanish, only -_ito_ is regularly appreciative.

-ito/a	mujercita, Juanito, viejecito
-ón	notición (big news), sillón _____

4. **Pejorative** (despectivo). Spanish is especially rich in pejorative suffixes. Quite often, in addition to being generally negative, they convey the idea of ugliness, overabundance, or poor quality. The equivalent in English sometimes is expressed with the adjectives "miserable or worthless" as in "that miserable or worthless book."

-aco	libraco (miserable or worthless book)	libro _____
-astro	poetastro	
-ote/a	feote, amigote, narizota	_____
-ajo	latinajo	_____
-acho	amigacho, poblacho	_____
-ongo	bailongo	_____
-orro	ventorro	_____
-orrio	villorrio	_____
-uco	frailuco	_____
-ucho	calducho, cafetucho, pueblucho	_____

In analyzing these suffixes of attitude in Spanish, we are able to make some broad but helpful generalizations. If the first vowel of the suffix is high front, /i/, or mid front, /e/, the suffix is usually favorable. If on the other hand, the first vowel of the suffix is high back, /u/, or mid back, /o/, it normally carries a negative connotation. If the consonant(s) of the suffix is/are dental or alveolar, the suffix is generally diminutive and appreciative. If the consonants are velar, palatal, or trills, the suffix is usually augmentative and pejorative.

PREFIXES

In this section we will look briefly at a listing of common Spanish prefixes. Because most of them have Greek or Latin origins, they are closely related to similar English prefixes. In the exercises which follow, write the English equivalent of the prefix cited, and the English equivalent of the model term as well:

1. Prefixes of Greek origin:

anti-	anti-	antirreligioso	antireligious
aero-		aeródromo	
antropo-		antropología	
astro-		astronauta	
biblio-		bibliografía	
cripto-		criptografía	
etno-		etnología	
geo-		geología	
hecto-		hectómetro	
hemi-		hemisferio	
hetero-		heterodoxo	
hidr-		hidráulica	
icono-		iconoclasta	
idio-		idiolecto	
kilo-		kilómetro	
macro-		macrocosmos	
micro-		microbio	
ornito-		ornitología	
seudo-		seudónimo	
toxico-		toxicología	
zoo-		zoología	

2. Prefixes of Latin origin:

abs-		abstinencia	
ante-		anteayer	
circun-		circunferencia	
deci-		decimal	
inter-		internacional	
octo-		octosílabo	
omni-		omnipresente	
pos-		posguerra	
pre-		prehistoria	

retro-	_____	retroceder
ultra-	_____	ultramar
yuxta-	_____	yuxtaponer

3. A third kind of prefix is used extensively in Spanish America among girls in their early teens. It is an intensifier:

re-	(very)	rebueno
requete-	(very)	requetebién, requeteganada
rete-	(even more)	retebonito

EXERCISE

Let us now review the four derivational classes of suffixes of attitude, and include the prefixes we've just listed.

1. For the following list of words, how has the affix altered the meaning? What is the base or stem?

reyezuelo	diminutive, pejorative	rey
casucha	_____	_____
maquinilla	_____	_____
anteanoche	_____	_____
aldehuela	_____	_____
abuelito	_____	_____
gripazo	_____	_____
besico	_____	_____
mujerona	_____	_____
intercambio	_____	_____
retenada	_____	_____
kilogramo	_____	_____
narigón	_____	_____

2. Using the prefixes and suffixes we have examined in this section, create an appropriate example for each of the following:

-ada	_____	(meaning?)__
pre-	_____	_____
-ito	_____	_____
-azo	_____	_____
-ote	_____	_____

105

```
biblio-        ————————————————        ————————————
geo-           ————————————————        ————————————
-ucho          ————————————————        ————————————
-ón            ————————————————        ————————————
-ín            ————————————————        ————————————
```

COMPOUND WORDS

The last process which we shall discuss in
this chapter has to do with compound words.
While compounding is much more common in English
than in Spanish (houseboat, firefly, fireman, etc.)
the process does occur in Spanish. In this section
we shall examine the three most common types of
compounding in Spanish.

The first type, a COMPOUND NOUN (sustantivo
compuesto), is created when two independent
morphemes are joined in a single new word. In
Spanish the most common combination brings together a verb and a noun, as in pasatiempo
(pastime). Let us list a number of interesting
examples (all compounds listed are masculine
except where noted):

el abrecartas	letter opener	abre - cartas
abrelatas	can opener	————————
altavoz	loudspeaker	————————
alzapaño	curtain hook, tieback	————————
apagavelas	candle snuffer	————————
cortalápices	pencil sharpener	————————
	also alfilalápices and	
	sacapuntas	
cubrecama	bedspread	————————
cuentagotas	(eye)dropper	————————
guardabarros	fender (car, bike)	————————
	also guardafango (América)	
guardacostas	coastguard	————————
guardaespaldas	bodyguard	————————
lavaplatos	dishwasher (person)	————————
limpiabotas	bootblack	————————
limpiachimeneas	chimney sweep	————————
limpiaparabrisas	windshield wiper	————————
matamoscas	fly swatter	————————
matasellos	postmark	————————

picaflor	hummingbird	
pisapapeles	paperweight	
quitamanchas	clothes cleaner	
	also sacamanchas	
quitasol	parasol	
rompehielos	icebreaker	
rompenueces	nutcracker	
la sacabala	bullet-extracting forceps	
el sacaclavos	nail puller	
sacacorchos	corkscrew	
	also sacatapón	
sacamuelas	quack (dentist)	
tocadiscos	record player	
la trotaconventos	go-between, procuress	

A second kind of compounding creates COM-
POUND ADJECTIVES by combining a noun and an adjective in the following manner:

barbicano	gray-bearded	
	also barbiblanco	
barbiespeso	heavy-bearded	
barbilindo	dandified, effeminate	
	also barbilucio	
barbinegro	black-bearded	
barbiponiente	apprentice, one just	
	beginning to grow a beard	
	also barbipungente	
barbirrucio	grizzled beard	
boquiabierto	open-mouthed, stupified	
boquiancho	wide-mouthed	
boquirroto	chatterbox	
boquirrubio	babbling	
boquituerto	crooked-mouthed	
cariancho	broad-faced	
cariacontecido	woebegone, down in the	
	mouth. Also caridoliente	
carigordo	fat-faced	
malasombra	bore, pest	
maniabierto	open-handed, lavish	
ojimoreno	brown-eyed	
ojinegro	black-eyed	
ojituerto	cross-eyed	
ojizarco	(familiar) blue-eyed	
pelicano	gray-haired	

107

```
pelicorto        short-haired      _____
pelinegro        black-haired      _____
pelirrojo        red-haired        _____
pelirrubio       blond             _____
```

A third kind of compounding involves the combining of three or more morphemes, as in the examples which follow. This process is a much less common one than the previous two.

```
el correvedile      gossip                          _____
                    also correveidile
la enhorabuena      congratulations                 _____
   enhoramala       unluckily                       _____
el hazmerreír       laughingstock                   _____
   metomentodo      meddler                         _____
   quitaipón        ornament on donkey's harness
   sabelotodo       know-it-all                     _____
   subibaja         seesaw, teeter totter           _____
   vaivén           backward and forward motion,
                    comings and goings              _____
```

EXERCISE

In the final exercise for this chapter, let us first review the compound words that we have just examined, and then follow it with a group of exercises that will refresh the material from the entire chapter.

1. Almost all of the compound adjectives that we listed in the preceding pages relate to parts of the body: beard, mouth, face, hands, eyes and hair. With this in mind, how do you suppose one would express these concepts in Spanish?

```
bushy, joined eyebrows    _____
happy-eyed                _____
long-haired               _____
long-faced                _____
```

2. Divide these compound nouns into morphemes, and explain the apparent meaning and form of each:

el espantapájaros _____

el portamonedas   _____
los quehaceres   _____
el correveidile   _____

3. Explain the meaning of <u>morpheme</u> and <u>allomorph</u>
using the idea of pluralness in Spanish.

4. Create acceptable Spanish words by adding
these suffixes to stems: <u>-ante</u>, <u>-ero</u>, <u>-azo</u>,
<u>-uca</u>, <u>-ín</u>, <u>-ajo</u>, <u>-ense</u>, <u>-eño</u>.

5. What is the difference between an <u>independent</u>
<u>morpheme</u> and a <u>dependent</u> (or <u>bound</u>) <u>morpheme?</u>
Explain and give an example of each in Spanish.

6. What is the probable meaning of these words?:
<u>jamoncito</u>, <u>ecuatoriano</u>, <u>olmedo</u>, <u>plomero</u>, <u>biólogo</u>,
<u>empobrecer</u>, <u>batear</u>, <u>mujerona</u>, <u>kilogramo</u>, <u>retro-</u>
<u>vender</u>, <u>bananal</u>.

7. As part of vocabulary-building, my intermediate
level Spanish students are required to learn new
vocabulary by explaining or using it in acceptable
Spanish sentences. What follows is a selection
of a few of the more amusing "mistakes." Explain
what the correct response probably should be, and
which aspect of linguistics is causing the student's
difficulty (whether it be morphology, or phonology).
What would you do to try to eliminate such errors
in the class?

    1. PARAGUAS. "Personas que viven en Paraguay."
    2. ENSUCIAR. "El profesor ensucia el es-
       pañol por la noche."
    3. EL CATARRO. "Para mandar una carta
       necesito dinero y un catarro."
    4. EL CATARRO. "El hombre que me trae
       cartas y paquetes."
    5. JUICIO. "El bebe el juicio de naranjas."
    6. LECHERO. "El lechero es bueno en la
       ensalada."
    7. SOPORTAR. "Mis padres me soportan."
    8. VENDAR. "La casa fue vendada por mi
       vecina."
    9. EL RATO. "El gato comió el rato."

10. SACAR. "Me saco el pelo con una
        toalla."

SELECTED BIBLIOGRAPHY

Lázaro Carreter, Fernando. Diccionario de términos
    filológicos. Madrid: Gredos, 1971.
Narváez, Ricardo A. An Outline of Spanish Morph-
    ology. Formation of Words: Inflectional and
    Derivational. St. Paul: EMC, 1970.
Pequeño Larousse Ilustrado. Paris: Larousse,
    1967.
Ramsey, Marathon Montrose. A Textbook of Modern
    Spanish. Revised by Robert K. Spaulding.
    New York: Holt, Rinehart & Winston, 1965.
Real Academia Española. Esbozo de una nueva
    gramática de la lengua española. Madrid:
    Espasa-Calpe, 1973.

Chapter 4

INTRODUCTION TO TRANSFORMATIONAL GRAMMAR

INTRODUCTION

In the past twenty-five years, linguistics
has been greatly affected by transformational
grammar (gramática transformativa). While still
somewhat lacking in practical results, the terminology and basic theory have been finding their
way into textbooks, and so for that reason we
will introduce some of the basic tenets here.

Transformational grammar is a means of
generating sentences (oraciones), both interior
(deep structures—estructuras profundas) and
exterior (surface structures—estructuras super-
ficiales), and which contains a mechanism to
describe these sentences in a systematic way.

Through the use of rules for transformation,
one is able to change one structure into another
by adding, subtracting or rearranging the elements.

To break this definition into smaller
pieces, the most characteristic elements of
transformational grammar are:

1. The phrase structure rules (reglas de
estructura sintagmática) which contain
the formal description of the grammatical
structure of the sentences (the deep
structure—estructura profunda).

2. The transformational rules (reglas
de transformación) which generate the
actual sentences themselves (the surface
structure—estructura superficial).

3. The structural tree (árbol estructural)
which is used to graphically illustrate
the relationship between the deep structure
of a sentence and its surface structure.

111

A number of common symbols are used by transformationalists in transcribing both the structural tree and the phrase structure rules:

Español		English	
O	Oración	S	Sentence
→	Consiste en/ rescribe	→	Consists of
+	y	+	and
( )	Opcional	( )	Optional choice
{ }	Ha de hacerse una elección	{ }	Obligatory choice

In order to demonstrate how they may be used in actual practice, let us create a very simple grammar below:

1. O→FN + FV (Some linguists prefer O→SN + SV.)

1. S→NP + VP

2. FV→$\begin{Bmatrix} Vt + FN \\ Vi \end{Bmatrix}$ (Adv)

2. VP→$\begin{Bmatrix} Vt + NP \\ Vi \end{Bmatrix}$ (Adv)

3. Adv→$\begin{Bmatrix} Tiempo \\ Lugar \end{Bmatrix}$

3. Adv→$\begin{Bmatrix} Time \\ Place \end{Bmatrix}$

4. FN→ det + Sustantivo

4. NP→ D + N

5. Vt→ comió, canta, bebió

5. Vt→ ate, sings, drank

6. Vi→ durmió

6. Vi→ slept

7. Tiempo→ anoche

7. Time→ last night

8. Lugar→ aquí, allí

8. Place→ here, there

9. det→ la, esa

9. D→ the, that

10. S→ chica, canción,   N→ teacher, song, girl,
        profesora,   lemonade, tortilla
        tortilla,
        limonada

The ten rules reproduced here are transcribed in
the normal, formulaic manner customary in transformational grammar. To make sure that the
conventions of this system are understood completely, let us express them again in the following manner:

1. The SENTENCE (S) CONSISTS OF (→) a NOUN
PHRASE (NP) AND (+) a VERB PHRASE (VP). La
oración (O) consiste en (→) una frase nominal
(FN) o sintagma nominal (SN) y una frase verbal
(FV) o sintagma verbal (SV).

2. The verb phrase (VP) consists either of a
TRANSITIVE VERB (Vt) and a noun phrase plus an
optional ADVERB (Adv), or an INTRANSITIVE VERB
plus an optional adverb (Adv).

3. The adverb (Adv) consists of an ADVERB OF
TIME (Time) or an ADVERB OF PLACE (Place).

4. The noun phrase (NP) consists of a NOUN
DETERMINER (D) and a noun (N).

5-10. The remaining rules are understandable
as expressed.

From this set of rules, we are now able to
generate a number of acceptable sentences in
Spanish and in English:

1. The girl drank that lemonade (last night).

    S→ NP + VP

    VP→ Vt + NP + (Adv)

2. La chica bebió esa limonada (anoche).

    O→ FN + FV

FV→ Vt + FN + (Adv)

3. The teacher sings that song (there).

S→ NP + VP

VP→ Vt + NP + (Adv)

4. La profesora canta esa canción (allí).

O→ FN + FV

FV→ Vt + FN + (Adv)

5. The teacher ate the tortilla (here).

6. Esa profesora comió la tortilla (aquí).

7. The teacher slept (here).

S→ NP + VP

VP→ Vi + (Adv)

8. La profesora durmió (aquí).

O→ FN + FV

FV→ Vi + (Adv)

9. The teacher slept (last night).

10. La profesora durmió (anoche).

Unfortunately, the same set of rules will also generate a number of unacceptable sentences:

1. *The lemonade sings the teacher (last night).

2. *La limonada canta la profesora (anoche).

3. *The tortilla ate the teacher (there).

This discussion, and these examples of acceptable and unacceptable sentences have shown how the phrase structure rules work in creating

114

a grammar which is able to generate sentences.
It also has been shown that there is a need for
careful refinement of the lexical units inserted
into the system. For that reason, the system of
PLUS AND MINUS FEATURES comes into play, used here
to refine the individual elements of the sentences.
Nouns, for example, would be labeled <u>+ human</u>
(teacher, girl) or <u>- human</u> (song, lemonade, tortilla), and the verbs would be modified in the
same manner and would also be marked as past
or non-past, until the rules were developed to
the point so that only acceptable sentences would
be produced. Such a refinement is one of the
major tasks that linguists have been endeavoring
to provide in recent years.

EXERCISE

     Using the Spanish version of the system
just introduced, write a set of rules which
takes into account these sentences:

    1.   El cazador mató el ciervo en la selva.

    2.   El joven estudió la lección anoche.

    3.   Mi amigo gastó su dinero ayer.

The rules for your grammar include:

    1. O→ FN + FV
    2. FV→ Vt + FN + Adv
    3. Adv→
    4. FN→
    5. Vt→
    6. Tiempo→
    7. Lugar→
    8. det→
    9. S→

Write several examples of acceptable sentences
generated by your grammar:

    1.   El joven mató el ciervo ayer.
    2.   _____

3. _____
4. _____

Are there any unacceptable sentences which would
also be generated? Give some examples:

1. * _____
2. * _____
3. * _____

What modifications are necessary to prevent the
unacceptable sentences from being generated?

STRUCTURAL TREE

        In the previous section we saw how to use
the phrase structure rules to describe and to
generate a set of acceptable and unacceptable
sentences. Another very widely used device in
transformational grammar is the STRUCTURAL TREE
(árbol estructural), a graphic means of demon-
strating grammatical relationships and especially
of illustrating deep structures. A DEEP STRUCTURE
(estructura profunda) contains all the information necessary in abstract form for the complete
syntactic and lexical interpretation of the
sentence. Let us examine a pair of them now,
using sentences which were generated by our
model grammar (sentence #8):

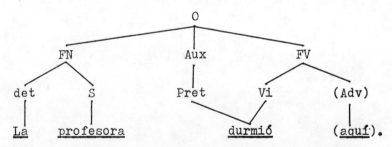

The structural tree enables us to see at a glance
the grammatical relationships of the sentence.
The use of the auxiliary (Aux) enables us to use
the preterit, since verb tense is one of the

116

functions of the slot/category. An additional
example follows using a sentence from our model
grammar (sentence #4):

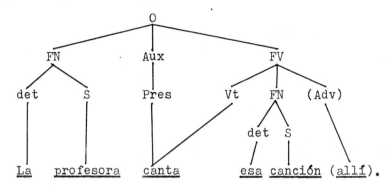

The structural tree is a metaphorical way of
describing the relationships between the various
parts of the sentence, revealing to us that the
farther one goes from the surface (in our examples,
the higher one goes from the model sentence),
the more abstract the deep structure.

EXERCISE

        Construct a structural tree for one of the
sentences generated by your grammar in the previous exercise:

        Your sentence:_____

        Structural tree:

117

COMPLEX SENTENCES

Complex sentences, consisting of sentences within sentences, are generally the result of EMBEDDING (incrustamiento). In describing this phenomenon, we approach it in such a way as to demonstrate with simple sentences how more complex sentences may be created. As an example, let us make two statements about someone and then combine them into a single sentence:

1. La profesora es inteligente.

2. La profesora enseña español.

One possible combination, as an example of embedding, is:

La profesora que enseña español es inteligente.

We may illustrate the deep structure:

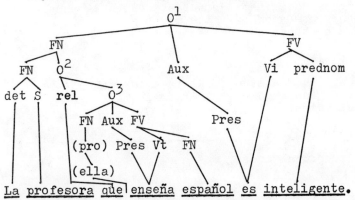

Another example of embedding may be shown by combining these sentences:

1. Juan no estudia mucho.

2. Juan es un chico listo.

We may combine them:

118

Juan es un chico listo que no estudia mucho.

In these examples, the two sentences are combined
into one by adding (rel), the relative clause
maker, que, and by eliminating all redundant
lexical items. The same procedure may also be
used to combine three sentences:

    1. La chica es bonita.

    2. La chica es mi vecina.

    3. La chica está en mi clase.

One possible combination of these three sentences,
eliminating redundancies, might be:

La chica bonita que está en mi clase es mi vecina.

What has been done here with three sentences
could also be done with four or more. Through
the process of embedding it is possible to expand sentences indefinitely, as in the well known,
". . . the house that Jack built."

EXERCISE

1. Try to create an additional example of an
embedded sentence by combining these two simple
sentences:

    El coche es amarillo.

    El coche está estacionado cerca de la esquina.

They may be combined into:

----

2. A more complex example:

    La biblioteca tiene miles de libros.

    La biblioteca es una parte de la universidad.

    La biblioteca está allí.

They might be combined into:

SUMMARY

In this very brief chapter it has been
our purpose to provide an introduction to the
terminology of transformational grammar and to
give some elementary examples of how the basic
processes function. The student interested in
pursuing this complex and fascinating study
should consult the excellent books listed in this
bibliography:

SELECTED BIBLIOGRAPHY

Hadlich, Roger L. Gramática transformativa del
        español. Tr. Julio Bombín. Madrid: Gredos,
Sánchez de Zavala, Victor, ed. Estudios de
        Gramática generativa. Barcelona: Labor,
        1976.
Stockwell, Robert P., J. Donald Bowen, & John
        W. Martin. The Grammatical Structures of
        English and Spanish. Chicago: U. of Chicago
        P., 1965.
Wardhaugh, Ronald. Introduction to Linguistics.
        New York: McGraw-Hill, 1972.

Chapter 5

PHILOLOGY (HISTORICAL SOUND CHANGES)

INTRODUCTION TO SOUND CHANGE PHENOMENA

In this chapter we will examine the Spanish language from a philologist's point of view, tracing the changes in form of a number of words through history. As embryonic PHILOLOGISTS (filólogos), often called HISTORICAL LINGUISTS, we know that all living languages change, and that all present-day languages have undergone changes in both sound and meaning. For that reason in this chapter we shall study the most important sound changes which contributed to making Spanish out of Latin.

Because the majority of sound changes are common to many languages, philologists have invented terms to name the processes. What we shall do here first is to list and define in alphabetical order the most important of these sound change processes so that the list may be readily consulted later for review. After that, we shall show the historical order in which they normally occurred in the development of Spanish, and follow this with enough exercises to enable the student to be able to analyze most words. Before beginning the list, however, a note about some of the conventions which will be used:

> means develops into.

STARE capital letters are used for Latin.

estar lower case is used for Spanish.

In alphabetical order then, here are the most important terms:

1. ANALOGY (analogía). By analogy we mean that two or more words conform to

121

the same sound pattern when the historical
origin of one or more does not allow
normally for the pattern. STARE>estar,
SEDERE>ser and IDIRE>ir are the results
of normal sound change processes, but
analogy occurs when the first person
singular of the present tense becomes
estoy, soy and voy. The influence of one
(or more) has also influenced the other(s).
A second example may be seen in the development AUSCULTARE>escuchar, in which
the AU of Latin normally develops into
o in Spanish, but because of analogy with
numerous other words which begin with es-,
the normal sound change pattern has been
disrupted.

2. APHERESIS (aféresis). The dropping
of an initial sound or sounds, as in
ILLOS>los.

3. APOCOPE (apócope). The loss of the
final sound of the word, such as SOLE>sol,
or MISERIAM>miseria.

4. ASSIMILATION (asimilación). The influence of one sound upon another. There
are several kinds of assimilation:

> a. PROGRESSIVE ASSIMILATION (asimi-
> lación progresiva). It occurs when
> the first sound in a sound cluster
> influences the second, as in PALUMBA>
> paloma. The sound of the m has
> caused the b to disappear. In this
> example, and others, it is called
> progressive assimilation because the
> influence moves from left to right
> (when looking at the written text),
> or from the articulated sound to the
> sound which is changed or influenced
> and which comes afterward. In this
> particular example, the assimilation
> is also complete, in that the influenced
> sound disappears. Another example

122

of progressive assimilation, LUMBU>
lomo is complete as well because of
the disappearance of the influenced
sound.

b. REGRESSIVE ASSIMILATION (asimilación regresiva). It occurs when a
sound is changed in anticipation of a
sound which follows, as in MENSA>mesa.
Once again the assimilation is complete because the influenced sound,
the n, disappears, and it is regressive in that the influence is
from right to left (when looking at
the written text), or in that the
second element or sound dominates.
Another example, from the development COMPUTARE>contar, reveals the
process of regressive assimilation in
the last step from comtar>contar.
The bilabial nasal m becomes a
dental nasal n because of anticipation or dominance of the sound of
the t, a dental stop. (For a discussion
of these descriptive terms, see the
chapter on phonology, or consult the
glossary.) In the last example
above the assimilation is partial
because the influenced sound is
changed but does not disappear.

c. NON-CONTIGUOUS ASSIMILATION
(asimilación armónica or a distancia).
When two non-contiguous, unlike sounds
(usually vowels) become alike, as in
DIRECTU>derecho, the change is
called non-contiguous assimilation.
In this case, the i of DIRECTU
becomes e in derecho through assimilation.

5. CENTRALIZATION (centralización). One
of many possible terms given to the process
whereby high front or high back vowels
are centralized to mid-ones, as in CUPPA>
copa and PILU>pelo. In the first example,

123

the high-back vowel, u, is centralized to
a mid-back o. In the second example the
high-front ī is centralized to a mid-front
e, and the high-back u is centralized to
mid-back o, a common occurence for final
u in Vulgar Latin.

6. DIPHTHONGIZATION (diptongación). A
name given to the process of changing an
accented vowel into a diphthong, as in
ROTA>rueda, and FEL>fiel. In the first
example, the o diphthongizes to ue [we]
and in the second, the e diphthongizes into
ie [ye]. A characteristic of the historical
development of the Castilian dialect is
this diphthongization of stressed o and
stressed e.

7. DISSIMILATION (disimilación). The
process whereby like sounds become unlike,
as in ARBOR>árbol. The two r sounds in
ARBOR become r and l in árbol. A second
example is ROTUNDUM>rodondo in which the
expected result is *rodondo, but because
of dissimilation, an e has been substituted.
(It is also possible that this change may
be due to analogy with the great number of
Spanish words beginning with the syllable
re-, whereas very few begin with the
syllable ro-.)

8. EPENTHESIS (epéntesis). The introduction of a new sound into a word, as
for example, TONO>trueno. The sound of the
r is the new sound introduced through
epenthesis. Another example is TUA>tuya,
in which the y is epenthetic.

9. FRICATIZATION (fricatización). A
term used to describe the origin in modern
Spanish of the fricative allophones of
voiced stops, as in LATU>lado. Fricatization is the name of the last step in the
change from stop t [t] to fricative d [đ].
(It has also sonorized—see below.)

10. LEARNED and SEMI-LEARNED FORMS (forma culta, semiculta). These are terms applied to words which have not undergone the sound changes normally characteristic of the popular, common words of the Spanish language. Often a single word in Latin, such as COLOCARE, will be borrowed twice (or more) and will produce a popular word, colgar, and a learned one, colocar. On other occasions a Latin word such as PLUMBUM will show a composite result which is neither learned nor popular, as in plomo. The two u's have centralized and the b has been completely assimilated, but the retention of the unchanged pl cluster causes it to be described as semi-learned. In popular words, the pl cluster is palatal-ized to ll [y] or [ḷ]. (See below.)

11. METATHESIS (metátesis). This term is applied to the change within a word of the location of a sound (usually an r or an l). There are two main types:

    a. SIMPLE (metátesis simple). One sound changes its location within the word, as in SIBILARE>silbar, in which the l changes its position. (The i is lost through syncope—see below.)

    b. RECIPROCAL (metátesis recíproca). Two sounds exchange positions with each other in a word, as when PARABOLA becomes palabra. The l and the r exchange places (the o is lost through syncope—see below).

12. MONOPHTHONGIZATION (monoptongación). This term, similar in meaning to simplifi-cation, describes the process of change from diphthong to monophthong as for example in PAUCUM>poco. The change from the diphthong AU [aṷ] to the monophthong o is due to this process.

125

13. ORTHOGRAPHIC TRADITION (tradición
ortográfica). A phrase used to explain the
presence of a written letter which is no
longer pronounced, as the h in hombre and
the p in psicología. It also describes
the spelling irregularities caused in
preserving the sounds [k] and [g] before
an e or an i, in the historical developments, CASEUM>queso and SEQUI>seguir. In
both examples the letter u is introduced
because of the Spanish orthographic tradition.

14. PALATALIZATION (palatalización). A
term used to describe the creation of a
palatal sound where there was none before,
as for example in LACTEM>leche. The c
[k] represents a velar sound and the t
[t] a dental sound. In the course of
history this consonant cluster became
simplified into a single sound whose
place of articulation is located midway
between the velum and the teeth (it has
become a palatal sound represented orthographically by ch [č]). This process then
is called palatalization, and in this
example, also simplification. An additional
example may be noted in PLORARE>llorar
where the pl consonant cluster is again
simplified into a single palatal sound
(represented orthographically by ll and
pronounced [y] or [l] in modern Spanish.
(See below.)

15. PROTHESIS (prótesis). A term used
to describe the process of adding a sound
to the beginning of a word, as for example
SPATHA>espada, in which the e is prothetic.
A characteristic of Spanish is the tendency
to add a prothetic e at the beginning of
any word which begins with a consonant
cluster consisting of s followed by a stop,
as in SCHOLAM>escuela (the CH in Latin
represented the sound [k]), and STELLAM>
estrella. In the second example here,
the e in modern Spanish is prothetic, and
the r is epenthetic.

126

16. SIMPLIFICATION (simplificación).
Sometimes called complex assimilation,
this term describes the combining of two
sounds into a third, as for example PAUCUM>
poco, in which the diphthong AU is simplified into a single new sound o. A second
example, serving to distinguish simplification from monophthongization is SIGNA>
seña, in which the consonant cluster GN
is simplified into ñ (which because the
result is the palatal ñ, the process may
also be labeled palatalization). At the
risk of adding potential confusion to the
issue, because the resultant Spanish sounds
in both of the examples above have places
of articulation midway between those of the
two parts of the Latin group, the process
may also be called centralization. However, to avoid this confusion as much as
possible, we will use centralization only
with reference to vowels.

17. SONORIZATION (sonorización). A term
used to describe the process of voicing
an unvoiced sound, as for example AMICUM>
amigo, in which the c [k] has become
voiced to [g] and which in modern Spanish
has developed into the voiced fricative [g].
Additional examples of sonorization include
TOTU>todo and CEPULLA>cebolla. In the
first example the t sonorizes to d and
then through fricatization becomes the
fricative [đ], while in the second example
the p sonorizes to b which then becomes
the fricative [ƀ].

18. SUBSTRATUM (sustrato). The influence
of the pre-Roman languages on the development of Latin has been termed the effect
of the substratum (the influence of one
language) or substrata (the influence of
two or more languages). Perhaps the most
well-known manifestation of the influence
of the substratum in Spanish is the loss
of initial f, as in the examples, FAMINEM>

127

hambre and FATUM>hado. In both of these
examples the modern spelling preserves the
orthographic tradition (see above). This
process of development is sometimes abbreviated with the formula f>h>∅, which
explains that f historically developed into
h which then became nothing (∅). The
fricative allophones of the voiced stops
are also thought to be caused by the influence of the substratum (see Chapter 1).

19. SYNCOPE (síncopa). A term used to
describe the process whereby a sound or
group of sounds is lost from within a word,
as in the example CALIDUS>caldo, in which
the sound of the i has been lost through
syncope. Another even more extreme example
is seen in COMPUTARE>contar, where the
whole syllable PU has been lost (this loss
of a whole syllable within a word is often
called haplology).

20. VOCALIZATION (vocalización). A term
used to describe the process whereby a
consonant becomes a vowel, as for example
CAPITALE>cabdal>caudal. Vocalization
occurs when the b of cabdal (a medieval
form of the word) becomes u, pronounced
[u] in caudal [kau̯dál].

For even greater ease of consultation,
we reproduce below a chart naming the processes
we have just defined with one or two examples
of each:

Name of Process	Examples (affected sounds are underlined)
1. Analogy	AUSCULTARE>escuchar estoy, voy, soy
2. Apheresis	ILLOS>los
3. Apocope	SOLE>sol MISERIAM>miseria

128

Process	Examples
4. Assimilation	
Progressive	PALUMBA>paloma LUMBU>lomo
Regressive	MENSA>mesa COMPUTARE>comtar>contar
Non-contiguous	DIRECTU>derecho
5. Centralization	CUPPA>copa PILU>pelo
6. Diphthongization	ROTA>rueda FEL>fiel
7. Dissimilation	ARBOR>árbol ROTUNDUM>redondo
8. Epenthesis	TONO>trueno TUA>tuya
9. Fricatization	LATU>lado [t]>[d]
10. Learned form	COLOCARE>colocar
Semi-learned	PLUMBUM>plomo
11. Metathesis	
Simple	SIBILARE>silbar
Reciprocal	PARABOLA>palabra
12. Monophthongization	PAUCUM>poco
13. Orthographic tradition	HOMINEM>hombre
14. Palatalization	LACTEM>leche PLORARE>llorar
15. Prothesis	SPATHA>espada SCHOLAM>escuela

Process	Examples
16. Simplification	SIGNA>seña
17. Sonorization	AMICUM>amigo TOTŪ>todo
18. Substratum	FAMINEM>hambre
19. Syncope	CALIDUS>caldo
Haplology	COMPUTARE>contar
20. Vocalization	cabdal>caudal

Let us now try to put these terms to work in the exercise which follows.

EXERCISE

Name the processes called for in each example:

Model: DOMINUS>dueño

a. The s disappears because of apocope.
b. The u centralizes to o.
c. The ĭ disappears because of syncope.
d. The m and n combine because of palatalization, and simplification.
e. The o becomes ue [we] because of diphthongization.

1. INSULA>isla

a. The u disappears because of s _____
b. The n disappears because of r _____
   a _____. In this case the
   a _____ is also complete.

2. BELLUS>bello

a. The s disappears because of a _____
b. The u becomes o because of c _____
c. The two l's combine into a single palatal sound through _____

130

3. **PERICULUM>peligro**

   a. The m disappears because of a_____
   b. The second u becomes o because of ____
   c. The first u disappears because of s___
   d. The c becomes g through s_____, and
      is now a fricative because of f____
   e. The l and r exchange positions through
      r_____ m_____

4. **SEMPER>siempre**

   a. The first e becomes ie [ye] through d___
   b. The second e and the r exchange posi-
      tions through _____ _____

5. **PAUPEREM>pobre**

   a. The m disappears because of _____
   b. The first e disappears because of _____
   c. The second p becomes b because of _____
      and later becomes a fricative because
      of _____
   d. The AU combination becomes o through __

6. **CONSUETUDINEM>costumbre**

   a. The m disappears because of _____
   b. The i disappears because of _____
   c. The first n disappears because of r____
      a_____
   d. The ue disappears because of _____
   e. The d becomes an n because of r____ a___
   f. The nn combination then becomes mn
      because of d_____
   g. The mn combination becomes mr because
      of d_____ (again!)
   h. The b is introduced by e_____

7. **MAGISTER>maestro**

   a. The e and the r exchange positions
      because of r_____ m_____
   b. The i becomes e because of c_____
   c. The g disappears because of _____

131

     d.   The final <u>e</u> becomes <u>o</u> through <u>a</u>_____
            with the large number of other words
            that end in the letter <u>o</u>.

8. <u>MACULA>mancha</u>

     a.   The <u>u</u> disappears because of _____
     b.   The <u>n</u> is introduced through <u>e</u>_____
     c.   The <u>cl</u> combination becomes <u>ch</u> [č] because
          of <u>p</u>_____ or simplification.

VULGAR LATIN

The language spoken by the Roman soldiers
and citizens who came to dominate the life of
the Iberian Peninsula is known to us today as
<u>Vulgar Latin</u> (Latín vulgar). Because it was a
spoken language not used regularly in formal
written documents, the reconstruction of it is
largely conjectural due to a lack of documentary
confirmation for many of the hypotheses.

Certainly one of the most important single
documents used in analyzing Vulgar Latin is the
<u>Appendix Probi</u>, a word list which was attached
to the <u>Instituta Artium</u> of Valerius Probus and
which dates from about the third century AD.
It contains a mere 227 items for which the correct
form is given for a number of common "mistakes,"
such as "VINEA non VINIA." While the main concern
of the author of the <u>Appendix Probi</u> was with
correct spelling, the corrections and the errors
give us a great deal of help in understanding how
Classical Latin developed into the Romance Languages. Through it and other similar documents,
including as well those written unconsciously in
Vulgar Latin, we are able to make some clear
distinctions between it and Classical Latin.

We know that Classical Latin made use of
long and short vowels. and that it showed phonemic
contrast between them by duration of articulation
rather than by stress as became the case in Vulgar
Latin. The Classical Latin vowel system contained
10 vowels: $\bar{a}$, $\breve{a}$, $\bar{e}$, $\breve{e}$, $\bar{\imath}$, $\breve{\imath}$, $\bar{o}$, $\breve{o}$, $\bar{u}$, $\breve{u}$. These
ten vowels developed into 7 in late Vulgar Latin,

as may be seen in this chart:

Classical Latin	Vulgar Latin	Late Vulgar Latin
Ă	a̦*	a
Ā	a̧*	a
Ĕ	e̦	e̦
Ē	ȩ	ȩ
Ĭ	i̦	ȩ
Ī	i̧	i
Ŏ	o̦	o̦
Ō	o̧	o̧
Ŭ	u̦	o̧
Ū	u̧	u

*The common diacritical marks used in discussing Vulgar Latin are:

a̦   Indicates an "open" letter, one having a more-open air passage.

a̧   Indicates a "closed" letter, one having a less-open air passage; the tongue is closer to the roof of the mouth.

ACCENTED VOWELS

The changes from Classical Latin to Vulgar Latin which have just been introduced are true of accented vowels, of syllables receiving primary and secondary stress. Those vowels which were part of unstressed syllables tended to disappear through syncope, as did the u̲ in SPATU̲LAM>espalda.

The ten vowels of Classical Latin, after

133

becoming seven in late Vulgar Latin, then developed into five vowels and two diphthongs in modern Spanish in this manner:

Classical Latin	Late Vulgar Latin	Modern Spanish	Example of Process
Ă	a	a	PĂTRE>padre
Ā	a	a	PRĀTU>prado
Ĕ	ẹ	ie	BĔNE>bien
Ē	ẹ	e	TĒLA>tela
Ĭ	ẹ	e	PĬLU>pelo
Ī	i	i	FĪCU>higo
Ŏ	ọ	ue	PŎRTA>puerta
Ō	ọ	o	TŌTU>todo
Ŭ	ọ	o	CŬPPA>copa
Ū	u	u	MŪLA>mula

We may summarize the information contained in this chart by saying that all the long vowels of Classical Latin as well as short-a remained unchanged into Spanish. Short-e and short-o became diphthongs while short-i and short-u centralized to e and o respectively.

We may show this graphically by putting only the short vowels of Classical Latin into a vowel triangle, and showing with arrows the resulting vowels of modern Spanish:

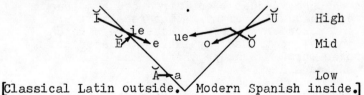

High

Mid

Low

[Classical Latin outside. Modern Spanish inside.]

134

The high vowels centralized, and the mid vowels
diphthongized. This change in the articulation
of stressed short vowels was the normal pattern
in Castilla, and as we noted in Chapter 3, this
development explains the pattern of a good number
of verbs (such as contar and sentir).

YOD

Unfortunately, a large number of vowels
develop in ways that do not conform to the pattern
we have just outlined, and in many cases the reason
for their failure to develop accordingly is the
YOD. The term is derived from the Hebrew name of
the letter y and is used philologically to describe the letter i when it is used as a semiconsonant (RADIA>raya) or a semivowel (caldairo>
caldero). An additional meaning comes from its
use in describing a palatal sound which influences
the historical development of vowels (MULTU>
mucho). The palatal sound of the yod may be
clear (written as an i in PLUVIA>lluvia or as an
e in AREA>era, followed by another vowel) or
the yod may be hidden. By hidden we mean that
it is not represented by the letter i or the
letter e but is inferred or understood in those
situations as the Latin consonant clusters
CT [kt] of LACTEM and the LT of MULTUM. Both
clusters are later simplified and palatalized into
ch [č] of leche and mucho. In the first example,
the hidden yod comes into play due to the raising
effect of the cluster—the C [k] is a velar
sound and the T is a dental—both are made with
the tongue high in the mouth. Because the tongue
is close to the roof of the mouth for both elements
of the cluster, only a small slip would be necessary to produce a palatal sound, and as history
has revealed, this is exactly what has happened.
Other similar hidden yods are found in the Latin
clusters GN, X [ks] and CL [kl].

The problem of the yod arises from the fact
that it causes certain changes in the historical
development of vowels, either raising them or
preventing them from becoming diphthongs. The

135

main features of the YOD are these:

1. Short-a̲ followed by a palatal (yod) becomes e̲:

>   FĂCTUM>hecho
>   ĀXE>eje

2. Short-a̲ followed by a consonant, followed by
the yod (represented either by the letter i̲ or by
the letter e̲ followed by another vowel) becomes e̲:

>   PRIMĂRIU>primero

>   > THIS PATTERN IS NORMAL FOR MOST WORDS
>   > HAVING: Ā + CONSONANT + YOD, and is
>   > historically documented as follows:
>   >
>   > PRIMĂRIU>primairu>primairo>primero.

>   ĂREA>era

3. Short-e̲ and short-o̲ followed by the yod do
not diphthongize:

>   PĔCTU>pecho
>   FŎLIA>hoja

>   > The modern Spanish articulation of
>   > the j̲ [x] is the result of fricati-
>   > zation and velarization. By VELARI-
>   > ZATION is meant that the point of
>   > articulation of a sound is changed
>   > so that it becomes velar.

4. Short-i̲ and short-u̲ followed by yod remain:

>   PĬCTURA>pintura
>   LŬCTA>lucha

5. The o̲ followed by a consonant followed by
yod becomes u̲:

>   morio>murió
>   POLIRE>pulir
>   POLLOCATA>pulgada
>   POLYPUS>pulpo

6. We may add to this discussion of short vowels that LONG-e followed by a consonant followed by yod, becomes i̱:

    CĒREU>cirio
    SĒPIA>jibia

The effect of the yod may be visually summarized in the following vowel triangle (once again, Classical Latin on the outside and modern Spanish on the inside):

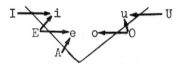

    Let us abbreviate all this information in a single formulaic chart which will show a definition and an example of each of the six uses of the yod:

RULE OF THE YOD	EXAMPLE
1. Ă + yod > e	FĂCTUM>hecho
2. Ă + consonant + yod>e	PRIMĂRIU>primero
3. Ĕ + yod > e	PĔCTU>pecho
Ŏ + yod > o	FŎLIA>hoja
4. Ĭ + yod > i	PĬCTURA>pintura
Ŭ + yod > u	LŬCTA>lucta
5. Ŏ + consonant + yod>u	PŎLIRE>pulir
6. Ē + consonant + yod>i	CĒREU>cirio

Historically the raising of the tongue to produce the yod also has had the effect of raising the preceeding vowels or of preventing their diphthongization.

EXERCISE

    To practice the material learned in this section, let us pause once again to do a short

137

exercise of the same type done earlier in the chapter.

1. <u>LACTEM>leche</u>

    a. The <u>m</u> disappears because of _____
    b. The <u>ct</u> cluster becomes <u>ch</u> [č] because of__
    c. The <u>a</u> becomes <u>e</u> because of centrali-
        zation caused by the _____

2. <u>CASEUM>queso</u>

    a. The <u>m</u> disappears because of _____
    b. The <u>u</u> becomes <u>o</u> because of _____
    c. The <u>e</u> and the <u>s</u> reverse positions because
        of _____ or due to the <u>y</u>
    d. The <u>ae</u> diphthong simplifies to <u>e</u> because
        of the influence of the <u>y</u>
    e. The modern spelling <u>qu</u>, pronounced [k]
        represents the continuing <u>o   t</u>

3. <u>BASIARE>besar</u>

    a. The <u>e</u> disappears because of _____
    b. The <u>s</u> and <u>i</u> reverse positions because
        of _____ or due to the influence
        of the <u>y</u>
    c. The <u>ai</u> diphthong simplifies to <u>e</u>
        because of the influence of the _____

CHRONOLOGY OF SOUND CHANGES

        In order to establish an approximate sequence
of these sound changes, in the following section
we have simplified and abbreviated the information found in Ramón Menéndez Pidal's classic
study, <u>Manual de gramática histórica española</u>
(Rpt. Madrid: Espasa-Calpe, 1968), pages 171-73.
In chronological order then, the major steps in
the development from Latin to Spanish include:

1. APOCOPE OF FINAL M. Very early, probably
even before the Romans completed the conquest
of the Iberian Peninsula in 46 AD., the final
<u>m</u> of most Latin accusatives had been lost.

138

(The accusative form had become the most commonly used form, and this simplification process was carried even farther so that it became commonplace to use FACTU instead of FACTUM and LACTE instead of LACTEM.)

2. VOWELS. The ten quantitative vowels of Classical Latin (distinguished phonemically by length) became seven qualitative vowels in Vulgar Latin (distinguished phonemically by stress and by place of articulation).

3. YOD. PACTE(M) becomes PECTU, which soon develops into pecho. MATERIA(M) retains the e̱ and permits the later development into madera.̱ At this stage only the vowels are influenced.

4. YOD. Disappearance of the above yod through palatalization of dental and velar consonants, as in RATIONE(M) [ratsyone] and PACE(M) [pakse]. It is the influence of the raising of the tongue here, often described as the "hidden yod."

5. SYNCOPE. Disappearance of intervocalic voiced stops and fricatives, as for example SARTA(G)INE and PROBA(V)I.

6. SONORIZATION. The sonorization of unvoiced intervocalic stops. as in DOMINICU(M)>dominigo> domingo, in which the c̱ is sonorized (voiced) to g̱ (and which later becomes a fricative [g] in modern Spanish). Another example is VICINITATE(M)> vicinidade>vecindad, in which the two ṯ's sonorize (and eventually become fricatives in modern Spanish).

7. SIMPLIFICATION. Simplification and assimilation of consonant clusters in examples such as SEPTE(M)>sette>siete, and URSU>oso.

8. VOCALIZATION. Vocalization of the ḻ in consonant clusters, as for example in the development of ALTARIU(M)>otero where one of the intermediate stages must have been *autairo, where the ḻ had vocalized to u̱.

9. VOWELS. The open-o̲ followed by yod does not diphthongize in the dialect of Castilla. Observe FOLIA(M)>hoja and SPOLIU(M)>despojo.

10. DIPHTHONGIZATION. Diphthongization of accented open-e̲ and open-o̲ (not followed by yod), as in JOCUM>juego and METU(M)>miedo.

11. PALATALIZATION. The simplification into single palatals of several consonant clusters, as in PUGNU(M)>puño, CULTELLU(M)>cuchillo, SPECULU(M)> espejo and RADIU(M)>rayo.

12. VOWELS. Syncope of pre-tonic and postonic vowels (those before and after the accented syllables), as for example PAUPERE(M)>pobre. (At this time the first e̲ is lost.)

13. YOD. Metathesis and simplification of the suffix -ARIA(M) into -era, in this manner: RIPARIA(M)>*ribaira>ribeira>ribera. Also palatalization of consonant clusters, as in LACTE(M)> leche.

14. CENTRALIZATION. Centralization of final u̲ to o̲, as in the development of PAUCU(M)>poco.

15. MONOPHTHONGIZATION. Monophthongization (or simplification) of diphthongs, as in AURICULU(M)> oreja.

16. APOCOPE. Apocope of final e̲, as in PACE(M)> paz and PANE(M)>pan.

17. VOCALIZATION. Vocalization of l̲, b̲ and p̲ in clusters created by a previous syncope, as in CALICE(M)>cauce and DEBITE(M)>deuda.

Changes 1 through 11 took place in Vulgar Latin, with those from 9 to 11 marking the transition between Latin and Romance. The most important landmarks of the sequence, in order, are:

1. Changes in vowels from ten marked by

140

quantity to seven marked by intensity and place of articulation. This forms the major step indicating the development of Classical Latin into Vulgar Latin.

2. Sonorization of intervocalic voiceless stops, marking the development into Romance.

3. Syncope of unaccented vowels. An important step in the early development of Spanish.

4. Loss of final e. A late but important moment in the development of Spanish.

EXERCISE

Let us now demonstrate that all the material of the chapter has been assimilated by doing a final exercise of the same type as before, but now restricting ourselves to the chronology suggested above:

1. CIVITATEM>ciudad.

    a. The m disappears because of a _____
    b. The two t's s _____
    c. The second i disappears because of s ____
    d. The v vocalizes to u
    e. The final e disappears because of a ____

2. MEDIETATEM>mitad

    a. The m _____
    b. The two t's _____
    c. The first e is influenced by the i (yod) and becomes ei because of metathesis.
    d. The unstressed syllable, de, now disappears because of hap _____
    e. The ei _____
    f. The first d becomes t through dissimilation.
    g. The final e _____

3. AUDITUM>oído

141

a. The m _____
b. The t _____
c. The d ι _____
d. The final u _____
e. The au _____

4. PROMPTUM>pronto

a. _____
b. The second p _____
c. The m _____
d. _____

5. CONSUETUDINEM>costumbre

a. _____
b. The i _____
c. The ue _____
d. The first n _____
e. The d becomes n as a result of r _____
f. The nn cluster then becomes mn and
   later mr because of d _____
g. The b is introduced _____

6. LACTUCAM>lechuga

a. _____
b. The first a _____
c. _____
d. The ct _____

7. OFFOCARE>ahogar

a. The c
b. The two f's become one
c. The first o becomes a because of a _____
   or perhaps because of d _____
d. The e
e. The f becomes h

8. CALAMELLUM>caramillo

a. _____
b. The ll
c. The e
d. The u
e. The l becomes r

142

9. HOSPITEM>huésped

    a. <u>m</u>
    b. <u>t</u>
    c. <u>i</u>
    d. <u>o</u>
    e. <u>e</u>
    f. <u>h</u>

10. PLICARE>llegar

    a. <u>c</u>
    b. <u>i</u>
    c. <u>pl</u>
    d. <u>e</u>

Now try to do all the steps in order, without the clues:

11. AUSCULTARE>escuchar (4 steps)

    Note: os->es- because of a_____

12. REGULA>reja (3 steps)

    Note: <u>ll</u> to <u>j</u> [x] is velarization.

13. MAXILLAM>mejilla (5 steps)

    Note: x [ks]>[š] and later>j [x] through velarization (2 steps)

14. RECUPERARE>recobrar (4 steps)
15. SARTAGINEM>sartén (4 steps)
16. PLANCTUM>llanto (4 steps)
17. LITTERARIUM>letrero (7 steps)
18. AUTUMNALE>otoñal (5 steps)

SELECTED BIBLIOGRAPHY

Canfield, D. Lincoln, and J. Cary Davis. An Introduction to Romance Linguistics. Carbondale: Southern Illinois Univ. P., 1975.

Corominas, Joan. _Breve diccionario etimológico de la lengua castellana_. Madrid: Gredos, 1967.

Corominas, Joan. _Diccionario crítico etimológico de la lengua española_. 4 vols. Madrid: Gredos.

Elcock, W. D. _The Romance Languages_. London: Faber & Faber, 1960.

Gili Gaya, Samuel. _Nociones de gramática histórica española_. Rpt. Barcelona: Bibliograf, 1966.

Lázaro Carreter, Fernando. _Diccionario de términos filológicos_. Rpt. Madrid: Gredos, 1971.

Menéndez Pidal, Ramón. _Manual de gramática histórica española_. Rpt. Madrid: Espasa-Calpe, 1968.

Lapesa, Rafael. _Historia de la lengua española_. Madrid: Escelicer, 1959.

Posner, Rebecca. _The Romance Languages: A Linguistic Introduction_. Garden City: Doubleday Anchor, 1966.

Spaulding, Robert K. _How Spanish Grew_. 1945 rpt. Berkeley: Univ. of California P., 1965.

Chapter 6

HISTORICAL SPANISH SEMANTICS

INTRODUCTION

In this chapter we are going to be dealing
with SEMANTICS (la semántica), the study of the
meaning of words. Our approach will be from a
historical point of view, focusing on ETYMOLOGIES
(etimologías), the scientific studies of the origin
and development of words. As the principal goal
of the chapter we shall attempt to outline some of
the major kinds of semantic change which have
influenced the development of the Spanish lexicon
from its Latin ancestor.

TYPES OF SEMANTIC CHANGE

There are a number of systems which one
might use to show the development of Spanish
semantics, but for our purposes the following
will provide a good outline of some of the
potentialities of semantic study. In many cases,
words remain virtually unchanged in meaning from
the time of their earliest usage. Those words
however which do change in meaning tend to change
in these basic ways:

1. BROADENING or EXTENSION OF MEANING
(extensión del significado). The modern
word has a meaning which includes the
former meaning but which has amplified or
enlarged its scope. For example, in Latin,
PERNA meant "thigh," whereas its modern
version in Spanish, pierna, means "leg."
That is, it encompasses all of the old
meaning but has enlarged it through the
process of broadening.

2. NARROWING or RESTRICTION OF MEANING
(restricción del significado). Sometimes
called SPECIALIZATION, it is the opposite
of broadening. Through narrowing, the
word has a restricted meaning in modern
times compared with its previously wider

one. To say it in another way, the modern
meaning usually is a specialized portion of
the former larger whole. A good example of
narrowing is the change in meaning from
Latin SECARE, "to cut" to modern Spanish
segar, "to harvest, to reap," in which the
modern meaning shows a specialization of
usage.

3. DISPLACEMENT THROUGH ASSOCIATION
(desplazamiento). Due to association with
a given activity, words often come to be
associated with a specialized part of that
activity, which then causes the terms to
assume a meaning that at times seem almost
unrelated to the initial meaning. Some
representative ways in which meaning may
be displaced include:

   a. PEJORATIVE (peyorativo). Because
   of association with some activity or
   state which is deemed unattractive,
   some words change in a negative manner
   and become PEJORATIVES, words which
   carry a negative or unpleasant meaning.
   A good example is the change by association of the Latin noun SINISTER, "the
   left side", with negative actions so
   that today the modern Spanish noun (like
   the English adjective as well), siniestro
   means "depravity, perversity." A
   second meaning of the adjective, siniestro, however, remains unchanged as
   "left, on the left side."

   b. AMELIORATIVE (ameliorativo).
   Because of an association with some
   activity or state which is considered
   attractive, favorable or commonplace,
   some words change their meaning in
   such a way as to soften the original
   meaning of the word. In some cases
   a negative word may become neutral,
   or a neutral one favorable. A good
   example of this change by association
   is the change from Latin ABHORRERE,

"to shrink back, to be averse to,"
to modern Spanish aburrir, "to bore
to weary." A very negative reaction
has become a more neutral one (and has
also been changed from passive voice
to active voice).

c. EUPHEMISM (eufemismo). Through
avoidance of certain tabooed acts or
words, a substitute is often found
which may be a metaphor of the original
term, or may be associated in some other
way with the forbidden term. A good
example of this is the change from the
Latin term SINUS, "curved or bent
surface," to the modern Spanish seno,
"breast." (This modern association,
however, was common in late Latin.)

d. METAPHOR (metáfora). Due to a
similarity of appearance or usage
some words acquire a metaphorical
meaning which associate it with that
activity or situation in the speaker's
mind. A good example of this kind
of metaphorical shift is found in the
origin of the modern Spanish word,
bigote, "mustache." It is derived
from the Germanic oath, "bi Got!" (By
God!), and came to be used to call
persons having a mustache—hence the
modern, bigote.

e. FOLK ETYMOLOGY (etimología popular).
A change in the form of a word as the
result of a popular notion of the origin of the term is caused by folk
etymology. Usually it causes a foreign
loanword or a word old enough to have
lost part of its original morphemic
clarity, to conform to the general
morphological pattern of the language.
For this reason, the word vagabundo
has become vagamundo in many Spanish
dialects because the morpheme -mundo
seems more meaningful for describing

147

one who wanders than does -_bundo_.

EXERCISE

The sketchy system we have just presented is only one of many possibilities. To test its validity, let us analyze the following list of words which have interesting etymologies:

1. BORRACHO. Derived in the late Middle Ages from _borracha_, "bota para el vino." It is a good example of 3d, DISPLACEMENT by METAPHOR. One might construe the change also as 3c, DISPLACEMENT by EUPHEMISM, since in both instances the change is brought about by substituting metaphorically one noun for another which is closely associated with it but which may also serve as a substitute for an earlier, less favorable term. One might argue as well that it is an example of 3a, DIS-PLACEMENT as a PEJORATIVE, since a neutral word, _borracha_, has taken on the negative aspects of _borracho_, "drunk, drunkard." This kind of complication is reasonably common, and is enough to let us know that we will be fortunate indeed when the change of meaning may be described in our system by one category only.

2. CHISTE. Derived from _chistar_, "to speak in a low voice," it was formerly associated with the kind of jokes that one tells in a low voice. In addition to 3b, DISPLACEMENT as AMELIORATIVE, the major part of the change should be classified _____ because _____ .

3. CHURRO, "finger-shaped fritters." A word of recent usage in this meaning since it dates from the nineteenth century. It is ultimately derived from an ancient pre-Roman term however, meaning "dirtiness, dirt; gross ones." In the major part of the change it is a good example of _____ because _____

4. GRINGO. An alteration of the word, _griego_, first used in the eighteenth century to describe one whose language was incomprehensible. After its first stage of development as 1, EXTENSION,

148

in which it came to be applicable to all foreigners, it has since changed to _____ because _____
To what group of foreigners does the word refer in Mexico? In Argentina?

5. AVEZAR, "to accustom, to be accustomed." Derived from Latin VITIUM, "defect, fault," the main change in meaning is _____ because _____

6. ARENGA, "harangue." Derived probably from Gothic *Harihrings, "a gathering (place)of the army." The change in meaning is primarily_____ because _____

7. CASA. From Latin CASA(M), "cabin, hut, cottage," the change in the modern meaning is primarily _____ because _____

8. CERROJO, "bolt." Derived in the Middle Ages from berrojo, "bolt," and influenced by the fact that it may be closed and by the similarity of the verb cerrar. This change in the form of the word is an especially good example of _____ because.

9. COLGAR. From Latin COLLOCARE, "to place, put in order, arrange," it is a fairly good example of the process _____ because _____

10. SALIR. From Latin SALIRE, "to jump, leap, bound." The change in meaning fits fairly well into the category _____ because _____

11. CURSI. "cheap, vulgar, flashy." Probably derived from Arabic, kúrsi, "an important per- sonage." The primary shift in meaning is _____ because _____

12. SABUESO, "bloodhound." From Latin SEGUSIUS, "bloodhound," but influenced in Spanish by sabe and hueso. This is a good example of _____ because _____

13. MANCEBA, "concubine." From Latin MANCIPIUM "slave," the primary change in meaning is _____ because _____

149

Now, using a good etymological dictionary such as Joan Corominas' _Breve diccionario etimológico de la lengua castellana,_ look up the origins of these words, and assign them to appropriate categories:

1. bodas   2. cosa   3. comadreja
4. bellaco   5. chaleco   6. chico
7. duelo   8. hogar   9. ropa
10. vianda   11. hermano   12. salpicar
13. siervo   14. siesta   15. quevedos

SELECTED BIBLIOGRAPHY

Corominas, Joan. _Breve diccionario etimológico de la lengua castellana._ Madrid: Gredos, 1967.
Corominas, Joan. _Diccionario crítico etimológico de la lengua española._ 4 vols. Madrid:Gredos.
Iribarren, José María. _El porqué de los dichos._ Rpt. Madrid: Aguilar, 1974.
Jeffers, Robert J., & Ilse Lehiste. _Principles and Methods for Historical Linguistics._ Cambridge, Mass.: MIT, 1979.
Kany, Charles E. _American-Spanish Semantics._ Berkeley: U. of California P., 1960.
Lapesa, Rafael. _Historia de la lengua española._ Rpt. Madrid: Escelicer, 1959.

Chapter 7

PROBLEMATIC GRAMMAR POINTS

For most linguistic discussions of the difficult features of Spanish grammar from the point of view of the English-speaking American student, it is wise to consult the landmark study of William E. Bull, <u>Spanish for Teachers</u>: <u>Applied Linguistics</u> (New York: Ronald, 1965). Using Bull's study as guide and reference, we shall combine with it the relevant features of traditional grammar texts in an attempt to present a clear and usable guide through four of the problem areas of Spanish grammar.

SER/ESTAR

Very early in the course of his or her studies, the American student of Spanish finds himself confronted with the problem of converting a single verb in English, <u>to be</u>, into two verbs in Spanish, <u>ser</u> or <u>estar</u>. The traditional manner of teaching the distinction is by listing a set of rules for using <u>ser</u>, usually from four to eight, and another set of rules for using <u>estar</u>, usually three to six.

Bull suggests that instead of teaching by long lists of rules, it is more economical to teach the student to think like a Spanish-speaking person—in this way the distinctions between the verbs are logical and not merely a matter of rote memorization. Certainly this point of view is admirable, but faced with the daily reality of large classes of only partially motivated students, we suggest that a combination of techniques often gives the best results.

Bull makes two major distinctions: <u>entity versus event</u>, and <u>change versus no change</u>. The first comes into play when one must make the choice of which verb to use to indicate location—the traditional answer is to say that location triggers the use of <u>estar</u>, as in the sentence,

151

<u>Juan está en Madrid</u>. As far as it goes, this
traditional rule will work for most situations,
but it fails to account for all the possibilities,
and for that reason creates a problem later on
when the student must relearn the rules at the
intermediate or advanced level in order to be
able to account for a sentence such as, <u>la boda</u>
<u>será en Madrid</u>.

Rather than contribute to this potential
confusion, Bull suggests that nouns may be
viewed as entities or events. Entities use <u>estar</u>
to indicate location: <u>Los Pirineos están en la</u>
<u>frontera entre España y Francia</u>; whereas events
use <u>ser</u>: <u>La reunión será a las once</u>, and <u>La</u>
<u>escena es en Madrid</u>.

A second important distinction noted by
Bull has to do with change versus no change,
and is useful especially in determining which
verb to use in sentences with descriptive adjectives. <u>Estar</u> is used to indicate change, and <u>ser</u>
to indicate no change. In this way then, the
difference between <u>Juan es gordo</u> and <u>Juan está</u>
<u>gordo</u> becomes clear and logical. In <u>Juan es gordo</u>,
<u>ser</u> is used to indicate no change; we know Juan
and expect him to be fat. If, on the other hand,
Juan normally is thin or perhaps even chunky, but
now appears changed in our eyes, we indicate this
change or changed <u>impression</u> in Spanish with the
verb <u>estar</u>. If we say, "María, .<u>Estás guapísima</u>
<u>esta noche!</u>," we are not insulting her—we are
conveying the idea of a changed impression, of her
being even prettier than usual tonight. In the
same way, <u>Jorge es enfermo</u>, suggests that Jorge
normally is sickly, while <u>Jorge está enfermo</u> conveys the idea that Jorge is sick (indisposed) only
for the present.

A third distinction which could conveniently
be added has to do with past participles. The
distinction between <u>ser</u> and <u>estar</u> here may well
be that of action versus result. For example,
<u>El ladrón es muerto (por el policía)</u>, conveys the
idea of the action—the thief is killed (by the
policeman). On the other hand, <u>El ladrón está muerto</u>

produces the idea that the thief is dead (as the result of the act of dying). Other pairs of examples may be seen to differ in the same way: <u>La chica es sentada</u> (she is led to a seat and guided to a seated position), and <u>La chica está sentada</u> (she is presently seated as the result of the act of sitting down). <u>El vaso es roto (por el muchacho)</u>, the glass is broken (by the youngster), and <u>El vaso está roto</u>, the glass is broken (into fragments), as the result of its being dropped or thrown.

The four final rules are structural and show <u>ser</u> to be used as a predicate nominative in linking: 1. noun and noun, 2. noun and pronoun, 3. pronoun and pronoun, and 4. adverb and adverb. Here are some examples of each type.

1. Noun and noun. Jaime es hombre; Carmen es mujer.

2. Noun and pronoun. (El) es profesor; (ella) es dentista. Es la una. Son las tres.

3. Pronoun and pronoun. (Ella) es la que lo hizo. (Ellos) no son los del grupo.

4. Adverb and adverb. Allí es donde vivimos. Por aquí es donde me robaron.

We may summarize this rule by the statement that <u>ser is used to link like-structures</u>.

EXERCISE

Apply these rules in the following sentences and determine whether <u>ser</u> or <u>estar</u> is to be used, and explain why:

1. La comida - - - en casa de Juan. Why?

2. Tu camisa - - - debajo de la cama.

3. La oveja - - - mansa.

4. ¡Qué joven - - - el viejo!

153

5. En el quinto piso - - - donde tengo mi habitación.

6. Las ruinas del templo - - - en México.

7. Los jóvenes no - - - los responsables en este asunto.

8. Veo que el pobre - - - herido.

9. ¿Cuál - - - la capital de Honduras?

10. Los dos - - - listos, pero hoy María - - - más lista que nunca.

11. Esta comida - - - muy bien preparada.

12. ¡Hombre! ¡Qué flaco - - -! ¿Has perdido veinte kilos?

PRETERIT/IMPERFECT

Again it is to William E. Bull's study that much of the enlightened linguistic discussion of the preterit/imperfect must be attributed. He was the first to formulate a graphic means of showing the distinction, which we have modified further:

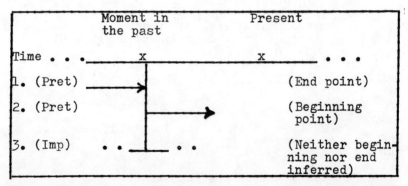

What this chart illustrates is the primary difference between the two aspects of the Spanish past. Arrow number 1 indicates an action which reaches an end point and is completed at a given moment in the

154

past (what Bull calls terminative), as for example, Ella lo comió. Arrow number 2 indicates the somewhat less common occurrence of an action beginning at a given moment in the past (what Bull calls initiative), as for example, Al verme, mi mujer siguió hablando con su amiga. Line number 3 conveys the meaning of the imperfect by showing that at a given moment in the past, the verb was neither at its beginning point nor at its end, as in the first verb in this sentence: Estaba lloviendo anoche cuando me desperté.

Bull's second set of distinctions, between cyclical and non-cyclical verbs is much more complicated than the equally satisfactory simple question, "Is it (the action or the state of being) completed?"

Good results may be achieved when the concept of two aspects of the past is taught first in English to beginning students so that they internalize the information that the past is divided into two kinds of actions or states: 1. those which are finished or completed, or 2. those which are not completed. This works well in the context of a brief narrative, such as:

> The sun was shining and the birds were singing this morning when my alarm rang and awakened me. I knew that I had to get up because I was going to take an exam. Despite the birds and the sun, I hated that clock for imposing itself on my dreams, but in the end, it was the clock that won the struggle of wills and forced me to get up . . .

By conveying the concept of the preterit/imperfect distinction in a narrative such as the one above, much of the ambiguity of simple isolated sentences often found in grammar texts is eliminated. Much less satisfactory is the typical model sentence, "They were eating when I arrived" (Ellos estaban comiendo cuando llegué). Sometimes the textbooks offer, Anoche llovió, as an example of a clear, completed past tense sentence, ignoring the fact

155

that <u>Anoche llovía</u> is also perfectly correct.
The truth is that neither example alone is satisfactory, but the combination of the two of them
is grammatically quite revealing.

For intermediate and advanced students,
the distinction between the preterit and the imperfect might well be presented using such minimal
pairs to show the terminative, initiative and
continuing aspects of the past. One such set of
instructional minimal pairs might be:

    1. Terminative versus continual.

<u>No pudo comprar la camisa.</u> (It was already
                               sold.)
<u>No podía comprar la camisa.</u> (The means to
                               buy it were
                               lacking.)
<u>Estuvieron allí.</u> (They got there.)
<u>Estaban allí.</u> (They were there.)
<u>Fuimos a la tienda.</u> (We arrived.)
<u>Ibamos a la tienda.</u> (We were on the way, or
                               went habitually.)

    2. Initiative versus continual.

<u>Supe la verdad.</u> (I've just become informed.)
<u>Sabía la verdad.</u> (I was aware of it.)
<u>Mi hija habló a los once meses.</u> (She began
    speaking at eleven months.)
<u>Mi hija hablaba a los once meses.</u> (She
           was already talking at eleven months.)

    3. Continual. (Expressions fixed as back-
ground information).

<u>Eran las tres.</u>
<u>Acababan de llamar.</u>

EXERCISE

1. As if you were going to teach the preterit/
imperfect distinction to a group of beginning
students, write a short narrative in English in
which you try to convey the differences as

clearly and simply as possible.

2. Explain the difference in meaning between these minimal pairs:

      María vio a Juan.
      María veía a Juan.

      El avión despegó a las seis.
      El avión despegaba a las seis.

      No quiso hablar conmigo.
      No quería hablar conmigo.

      Por la mañana hizo sol.
      Por la mañana hacía sol.

      Trabajé allí.
      Trabajaba allí.

PARA/POR

As with ser/estar and the preterit/imperfect, the correct usage of para and por requires that the English-speaking student make a choice between two possibilities in Spanish for a single one, "for," in English. In those situations requiring the meanings "by" and "through" in English, the student finds little difficulty in supplying por. In the same manner, English "in order to" produces Spanish para.

The difficulty is encountered in situations where English uses "for", situations like these:

      He went for bread.
      The gift's for you.
      She speaks Spanish well for an American.

What is needed is a means of explaining how Spanish divides the concept which is offered in English as "for." As with the preterit/imperfect distinction, this contrast too lends itself to a graphic interpretation:

<u>Para</u> tends to be a linear, one way directional
concept.

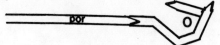

    Mañana salimos <u>para</u> México.
    La corbata es <u>para</u> ti.
    Los obreros trabajan <u>para</u> la compañía.
        (They supply their labor to the company.)
    Estamos <u>para</u> salir. (We're at the point of
        leaving.)

<u>Por</u> tends to convey a broader, reciprocal concept.

    El decano trabaja <u>por</u> la universidad. (He
        works on its behalf.)
    Lo hicimos <u>por</u> dos horas. (The duration of
        the capsule of time.)
    Porque estaba enferma, hicimos la tarea
        <u>por</u> ella.
    Estamos <u>por</u> salir. (Preparations are well
        in hand for leaving.)

This theoretical framework also seems to resolve
these examples:

    Este cuaderno no sirve <u>para</u> nada. (No
        reciprocity)
    Lo compramos <u>por</u> veinte dólares. (Reci-
        procity yes)
    Lo dejo <u>para</u> otro día. (Directional end
        point)

The division seems appropriate as we see in this
final set of minimal pairs:

    Mañana salimos <u>para</u> Detroit. (End point—
        destination)
    Mañana salimos <u>por</u> Detroit. (Broader
        concept—through)

El regalo es <u>para</u> mi madre. (Destination)
El regalo es <u>por</u> mi madre. (Reciprocal—
   on her behalf)

Es muy inteligente <u>para</u> político. (Inference
   that most aren't)
Es muy inteligente <u>por</u> político. (Inference
   that most are)

Luchan <u>para</u> la libertad. (Directional—
   they don't have it and are struggling
   to get it.)
Luchan <u>por</u> la libertad. (Reciprocal—they
   feel they have it and are fighting to
   defend it.)

Están <u>para</u> decir adiós. (At the point of
   saying it)
Están <u>por</u> decir adiós. (They're getting
   ready—broader concept)

EXERCISE

How would you translate these simple sentences
into Spanish? Explain why <u>para</u> or <u>por</u> was chosen
in each case. In the event that both are possible,
explain the difference in meaning:

1. <u>For</u> me? Thanks!
2. He plays the piano well <u>for</u> a child.
3. He lent me his car <u>for</u> a month.
4. I paid thirty-five dollars <u>for</u> that book.
5. My wife works <u>for</u> the university.
6. They're leaving <u>for</u> Madrid.
7. Watch my car <u>for</u> five minutes!
8. I need the money <u>for</u> tomorrow.
9. What is that tool used <u>for</u>?
10. She went to the store <u>for</u> milk and yogurt.

SUBJUNCTIVE

The subjunctive is the fourth of the grammar
problems we are examining in this chapter. It is
such a problem for many American students and teachers that in many classes in high schools, the
instructor somehow never manages to reach the

subject by the end of the term or the school
year. There is really very little reason for
this fear as we shall attempt to demonstrate in
this brief section.

Aside from direct commands such as, ¡Venga!,
¡No lo comas!, ¡Hablemos!, the subjunctive is
used primarily in subordinate clauses which may
function syntactically as a noun (clause), an
adverb (clause) or an adjective (clause), as we
see in these examples:

1. The subjunctive in subordinate noun clauses.

Queremos que nuestro amigo venga a vernos.

Es mejor que lo compre aquí que en otra tienda.

Me molesta que no estén aquí.

In all of these examples the subjunctive in
the noun phrase is found as a verbal comple-
ment (usually a direct object) and receives
the influence of the main verb expressing
influence, doubt or denial.

2. The subjunctive in subordinate adverbial
clauses.

Traigo el libro para que lo veas.

Iremos con tal que vengan ellos.

Aunque estudien mucho, no se cansarán.

The adverbial expressions also generate the
subjunctive by exerting influence, doubt or
denial on the verb which follows.

3. The subjunctive in subordinate adjectival
clauses.

Buscamos un señor que hable cinco idiomas.

Escogerá el disco que le guste.

No he conocido jamás un hombre que hable tanto.

In addition to these uses of the subjunctive in
subordinate clauses, the subjunctive may also
be used in main clauses in certain conditions:

4. Direct commands.

¡Venga!

¡No vayas con él!

5. With adverbs of doubt and desire.

Tal vez ya lo haya hecho.

Quizá le haya dicho el chisme.

¡Ojalá vengan pronto!

6. With si.

Si estuviéramos en Madrid iríamos a la
    Plaza Mayor.
Yo no sé lo que haría si tuviera un millón
    de dólares.

These six types of sentences are the major ways
the subjunctive is used in Spanish. We shall now
point out some of the most important governing
factors.

Once again Bull has offered some valuable
suggestions for simplifying the process. Perhaps
the most important of his suggestions about the
subjunctive is the contrast he offers between
anticipation and experience. This distinction is
especially valuable in sentences having subordinate
adverbial or adjectival clauses, as in the following examples: (ANTICIPATION uses the subjunctive;
EXPERIENCE takes the indicative)

ANTICIPATION

Busco un hombre que hable cinco idiomas.
    (We don't know who it is.)

EXPERIENCE

Busco al hombre que habla cinco idiomas.
(We know he exists.)

A(NTICIPATION)
Cuando beba, habla demasiado. (Anticipated, not a regular occurence)
E(XPERIENCE)
Cuando bebe, habla demasiado. (Experience, a regular occurence)

A. Estudiarán hasta que lleguen sus amigos.
E. Estudiaron hasta que llegaron sus amigos.

It may be seen here that many of the ambiguous cases for the English-speaking student are resolved by Bull's contrast between experience and anticipation (or non-experience). This concept is sometimes introduced in the textbooks as the idea of "future doubt," meaning that the main verb is of future intent and that the action of state of being related by the secondary verb has not yet transpired. Some more examples here show this quality of ANTICIPATION:

Comenzaremos en cuanto lleguen.

Seguiré sin tu ayuda mientras no me hables.

Aunque estén en la ciudad no vendrán a verte.

Si tuviera un carro nuevo iría a México.

If the ambiguous cases are resolved by Bull's contrast between anticipation and experience, let us complete our discussion by showing the unambiguous cases. The subjunctive is always triggered in a subordinate clause when the main clause verb or adverb exerts INFLUENCE, casts DOUBT OR DENIAL, or shows an EMOTIONAL REACTION. Here are some appropriate examples:

1. INFLUENCE.

Insisto en que me lo des en seguida.
Es importante que encontremos el recado.
Quiero usar el libro para que todos me entiendan.

162

2. DOUBT OR DENIAL.

>No es que lo sepa ella.
>No creo que tengan razón.
>Salimos sin que lo supieran.
>Es posible que estudien.
>Dudo que lo hayan hecho bien.

3. EMOTIONAL REACTION.

>Me alegro de que hayas gozado de la fiesta.
>Es bueno que hagan caso de lo que digo.
>Nos gusta que aproveches.

While the subjunctive remains a problem area for English-speaking students, using the basic guidelines given here, as well as sufficient practice to see the underlying logic behind them, most students should be able to handle the subjunctive well enough to cease the typical avoidance of the topic common in many high schools.

EXERCISE

1. Explain the reasoning involved in using the indicative or the subjunctive in these pairs of sentences:

>Creo que estudian.
>>No creo que estudien.
>Es seguro que lloverá en mayo.
>>No es seguro que nieve en noviembre.
>Nos saludan siempre que nos ven.
>>Nos saludarán siempre que nos vean.
>Nos sentamos juntos desde que llega hasta que sale.
>>Nos sentaremos juntos desde que llegue hasta que salga.
>Nos tostamos cuando hace sol.
>>Nos tostaremos cuando haga sol.
>Aquí hay alguien que quiere verte.
>>Aquí no hay nadie que quiera verte.
>Me refiero a los estudiantes que no han estudiado.
>>Me refiero a los estudiantes que no hayan estudiado.

163

Te digo que voy.
   Te digo que vayas.

2. Choose the correct form of the verb in these
sentences and explain why you have made the selection that you have.

   1. No es importante que tú (venir).
   2. Necesito que Ud. me (ayudar).
   3. Me agrada que ellos (haber) leído la
      lección.
   4. Conocemos a un carpintero que (saber)
      hacerlo bien.
   5. Hay que encontrar a alguien que (poder)
      contestar la pregunta.
   6. Hay niños que (hablar) a los diez meses.
   7. Lamento que tú me lo (haber) comunicado.
   8. Aunque yo (tener) coche no me gustaría
      conducir.
   9. Es evidente que él (ser) listo.
   10. Me lo ha vendido sin (saber)lo nadie.

SELECTED BIBLIOGRAPHY

Bull, William E. Spanish for Teachers: Applied
   Linguistics. New York: Ronald, 1965.
Fente Gómez, Rafael, Jesús Fernández Alvarez,
   & Lope G. Feijóo. El subjuntivo. Madrid:
   SGEL, 1972.
Politzer, Robert L., & Charles N. Staubach.
   Teaching Spanish: A Linguistic Orientation.
   Lexington, Mass: Xerox, 1965.
Ramsey, Marathon Montrose. A Textbook of Modern
   Spanish. Revised by Robert K. Spaulding.
   New York: Holt, Rinehart & Winston, 1965.
Terrell, Tracy D., & Maruxa Salgués de Cargill.
   Lingüística aplicada a la enseñanza del
   español a angloparlantes. New York: John
   Wiley, 1979.

BILINGUAL GLOSSARY OF LINGUISTIC TERMS

In this glossary virtually all of the linguistic terms used in the text will be defined again as simply and clearly as possible. In most cases the examples will be new and hence will supplement those found in the body of the text. Spanish terms are alphabetized along with English terms. Usually the English terms are the ones defined, while Spanish terms are given their English equivalents. For those terms which may require additional clarification or discussion, an appropriate chapter is indicated.

Acento de intensidad: Stress. Tonic accent.

Ademán: Gesture.

Aféresis: Apheresis.

AFFIX: (Afijo). A morpheme which is added to a stem at the beginning (PREFIX), at the end (SUFFIX) or in the middle (INFIX).

AFFIXATION: (Afijación). The process of adding an affix to a stem.

AFFRICATE: (Africado). A compound sound consisting of a stop plus a fricative. The first sound in chico [čiko] is an example. (Chapter 2.)

Afijación: Affixation.

Africado: Affricate.

ALLOMORPH: (Alomorfo). The individual variant of a morpheme in a given utterance Two allomorphs of the morpheme "plural" are: -/s/ as in manos, and -/es/ as in frijoles.

ALLOPHONE: (Alófono). The individual variant of a phoneme in a given utterance. Two allophones of the phoneme /b/ are noted in the word, embebido [embebido].

Alófono: Allophone.

Alomorfo: Allomorph.

ALVEOLAR RIDGE: (los Alvéolos). Sometimes called
the gum ridge, the alveolar ridge is the
roughened area of the roof of the mouth
between the teeth and the hard palate. In
Spanish, the /r/ of oro is alveolar.

Alvéolos: Alveolar ridge.

AMELIORATIVE: (Ameliorativo). A favorable change
in the meaning of a word. (Chapter 6).

Analogía: Analogy.

ANALOGY: (Analogía). The change in the form of
a word brought about by the influence of a
generalized pattern in the language. The
in- of invierno, from Latin HIBERNUM is the
result of analogy with other words in Spanish
that begin with the prefix in-.

APEX: (Apice). The tip of the tongue. The /t/
of lata is apicodental.

APHERESIS: (Aféresis). The dropping of an initial
sound, as in the historical development of
LECTORILEM>latril>atril (lectern).

Apice: Apex.

APOCOPE: (Apócope). The loss of the final sound
or sounds in a word, as santo>san and
COLOCARE>colocar.

APPLIED LINGUISTICS: (la lingüística aplicada).
The field of linguistics especially concerned
with improving foreign language education
through applying linguistic techniques.

APPRECIATIVE: (Apreciativo). An affix which
changes a word so that the word conveys a
favorable attitude, as does the suffix
-ito in the word abuelito. (Chapter 3).

Arbol estructural: Structural tree.

Arbol geneológico: Family tree (language family tree).

ARTICULATION: (Articulación). The production of meaningful sounds.

ARTICULATORY APPARATUS: (Los órganos de articulación). The movable and the passive organs which are used to produce meaningful sounds. The tongue is a movable organ, and the hard palate is an example of a passive one.

Asimilación armónica or Asimilación a distancia: Non-contiguous assimilation.

Asimilación progresiva: Progressive assimilation.

Asimilación regresiva: Regressive assimilation.

ASPIRATION: (Aspiración). The explosion of air which occurs in English after voiceless initial stops, as the p in Peter [p^{h}irəR]. (Chapter 2).

ASSIMILATION: (Asimilación). The influence of one sound upon another. The influence may be partial in that the influenced sound does not disappear, or complete when it does disappear. In a grouping of two sounds, when the first influences the second, it is called PROGRESSIVE ASSIMILATION, and when the influence is from the second sound to the first it is called REGRESSIVE ASSIMILATION. When the two sounds being assimilated are separated by an intervening sound or sounds it is called NON-CONTIGUOUS ASSIMILATION. (Chapter 5).

AUGMENTATIVE: (Aumentativo). An affix which produces an increase in the size or intensity of the stem, such as the suffix -ón in the word hombrón. (Chapter 3).

Aumentativo: Augmentative.

167

BASQUE: (Vasco/vascuence). The non-Indo-European language of the Basque people of northern Spain and southern France. It is thought by many to be related to the ancient Iberian language of pre-Roman times.

BLADE: (Lámina). The wide part of the tongue just behind the tip or apex.

BROADENING or EXTENSION OF MEANING: (Extensión del significado). A change in the meaning of a word which includes the former meaning as well as a newer more expanded meaning. (Chapter 6).

Cavidad nasal: Nasal passage or cavity.

CECEO: A term used in Spanish to describe the characteristic interdental pronunciation of Castilla wherein the z or zorro and the c of cero are articulated as the voiceless interdental fricative [θ].

CENTRALIZATION: (Centralización). The lowering of a high front or high back vowel resulting in a mid front or a mid back vowel, as in the development PILUM>pelo. (Chapter 5).

CLASSICAL LATIN: (Latín clásico). The quantitative language of ancient Rome formalized in literature and distinct from Vulgar Latin which is the ancestor of Spanish as well as the other Romance Languages.

CLITIC: (Clítico). A word added to the end of another. The word lo is a clitic when joined to ver in the sentence, Quiero verlo.

CO-ARTICULATED: (Co-articulado). When sound is simultaneously produced in two places of the mouth, the result is a co-articulated sound. In some dialects, un hueso is pronounced [uŋweso] so that the fricative [ǥ] is articulated at the same time as the [w]. (Some linguists transcribe this sound with the slightly different symbol, [ɰ].) (Chapter 2).

168

COMPLEMENTARY DISTRIBUTION: (Distribución).
When the allophones of a given phoneme or
the allomorphs of a given morpheme may not
occur in the same environment while at the
same time dividing all the possibilities
of the phoneme or morpheme between them,
they are said to be in complementary distribution. As an example, the two allophones
of the /d/ are distributed so that the stop,
[d] occurs after a pause or a nasal, while
the fricative [đ] occurs in all other positions. (Chapter 2).

COMPOUND NOUN: (Sustantivo compuesto). A noun
composed of two or more independent morphemes, such as abrelatas, from abre and
latas.

CONSONANT: (la Consonante). A speech sound produced by partial or complete obstruction of
the air passage.

Continua: Continuant.

CONTINUANT: (Continua). A general class of
consonant phonemes which permits the
continuous flow of the air stream. Examples include the /n/ and /m/ among others.

Cotejo: Minimal pair.

Cuerdas vocales: Vocal cords.

DEEP STRUCTURE: (Estructura profunda). Contrasting
with SURFACE STRUCTURE, the deep structure
corresponds to the underlying meaning of
a sentence. (Chapter 4).

DEPENDENT or BOUND MORPHEME: (Morfema dependiente).
A morpheme which may not occur independently
in an utterance, such as the plural morpheme,
-/s/ of hombres. (Chapter 3).

DERIVATION: (Derivación). The process of adding
a non-inflectional affix to a base or stem
in order to create a new word, such as

169

the suffix -ona added to mujer to make
mujerona. (Chapter 3).

Despectivo: Pejorative.

Desplazamiento: Displacement.

Determinante: Noun determiner.

DIACRITICAL MARKS: (Signos diacríticos).
Linguistic symbols used primarily in
phonology to indicate place or mode of
articulation. Examples include: [č]
(palatal), [t] (dental), [z] (interdental)
[đ] (fricative), [ñ] (palatal). (Chapter 2).

DIALECT: (Dialecto). The variety of a language
spoken by a group of people separated from
other speakers of the same language because
of geographical location or socio-economic
class.

DIALECT GEOGRAPHY: (Geografía lingüística).
The study of linguistic variations that
may be shown on a map.

DIALECTOLOGY: (Dialectología). The study of
dialects.

DIMINUTIVE: (Diminutivo). This results when a
derivational affix is added to a stem or
base, creating a word altered by the sense
of smallness. The suffix -cito creates
the diminutive ratoncito.

DIPHTHONG: (Diptongo). A compound vowel sound
consisting of a vowel plus a semiconsonant,
or a vowel plus a semivowel. The words
bien [byen] and seis [seis] contain diphthongs.

DIPHTHONGIZATION: (Diptongación). The process
(usually historical) of creating a diphthong
from a vowel, as in the example BONUM>bueno
[bweno], in which the o becomes ue [we].

170

Diptongo creciente: Rising diphthong.

Diptongo decreciente: Falling diphthong.

DISPLACEMENT: (Desplazamiento). Because of association with new circumstances, the semantic
value of a word becomes greatly altered.
(Chapter 6).

DISSIMILATION: (Disimilación). The process of
two like sounds becoming unlike, as in
CARCERE>cárcel, in which the two r's become
r and l. (Chapter 5).

Distensión: Off-glide.

DISTINCTIVE FEATURES: (Rasgos distintivos). The
system of describing sounds, morphemes and
words using plus and minus features.
(Chapter 2).

Distribución: Complementary distribution.

Dorso: Dorsum or Back of the tongue.

DORSUM: (Dorso) The back of the tongue. The
dorsum is used to articulate the initial
sound of casa [kasa].

EMBEDDING: (Incrustamiento). The process of
combining a sentence within a sentence,
usually introduced in Spanish by the
word que. (Chapter 4).

Elementos segmentales: Segmental features.

Elementos suprasegmentales: Suprasegmental
features.

Entonación: Intonation.

EPENTHESIS: (Epéntesis). The introduction of a
new sound into a word, as the b in the
historical development of HOMINEM>hombre.

Espirante: Spirant.

171

Estructura profunda: Deep structure.

Estructura superficial: Surface structure.

Etimología: Etymology.

Etimología popular: Folk etymology.

ETYMOLOGY: (Etimología). The study of the
    history and development of words.

EUPHEMISM: (Eufemismo). The substitution of an
    inoffensive term for one deemed offensive,
    as embriagado for borracho.

Extensión del significado: Broadening or Exten-
    sion of meaning.

FALLING DIPHTHONG: (Diptongo decreciente). A
    diphthong consisting of a vowel and a
    semivowel. An example is the diphthong
    ai [ai] in bailar [bailar].

Familia de lenguas: Language family.

FAMILY TREE: (Arbol geneológico). A graphic
    representation of the relationship between
    the parent language (Latin, for example),
    and the offspring (the Romance languages).

Filología: Philology.

FOLK ETYMOLOGY: (Etimología popular). The
    change in the form of a word as a result of
    a misconception of the origin or meaning of
    the term, or because of the influence of other
    words of morphemes thought to be analogous.
    In Spanish, berrojo has become cerrojo because
    of folk etymology. (Chapter 6).

Fonema: Phoneme.

Fonética: Phonetics.

Fonología: Phonology.

Forma culta or Cultismo: Learned form.

Forma semiculta or Semicultismo: Semi-learned form.

FREE VARIATION: (Variación libre). Two or more
    allophones of a single phoneme are said to be
    in free variation when they may occur in the
    same position or environment freely at the
    discretion of the speaker. The allophone [ŋ]
    is in free variation with [n] in the word
    Juan, before a pause. (Chapter 2).

FRICATIVE: (Fricativa). A consonant sound pro-
    duced by the construction of the air passage
    so that friction is produced. The g of
    hago is a fricative.

Fricativa alargada: Slit fricative.

Fricativa redondeada: Groove fricative.

Fricatización: Fricatization.

FRICATIZATION: (Fricatización). The process of
    creating a fricative out of a stop.

GENTILICIO: In Spanish an adjective or noun indi-
    cating racial or national origin is called a
    gentilicio. A number of morphological
    suffixes pertain to gentilicios, such as
    -teco in guatemalteco. (Chapter 3).

Gesture: (Ademán). See KINESICS.

GLOTTAL CLOSURE or BOUNDARY ELEMENT: (Golpe de
    glotis). A characteristic of English speech
    is a brief closing of the glottis before
    words that begin with a vowel, as in the groups
    (when carefully articulated), She opened
    angrily, and He ate apples. The glottal
    closure is a characteristic of moderately
    careful English speech, but it is foreign
    to Spanish and should be avouded. (Chapter 2).

Gramática transformativa: Transformational grammar.

173

GROOVE FRICATIVE: (Fricativa redondeada). The class of fricatives characterized by the groove-like shape of the constricted air passage created in the production of these sounds. The groove runs from the back of the mouth to the front. Two Spanish examples are the [s] in salsa and the [z] in asno.

Hamito-Semitic: The large family of languages which includes Arabic and Hebrew.

HAPLOLOGY: (Haplología). The loss of a whole syllable in the historical development of a word, as in COMPUTARE>contar, where the pu is lost. (Chapter 5).

HARD PALATE: (Paladar). The hard, bony part of the roof of the mouth between the alveolar ridge and the velum. The /č/ is a palatal phoneme in Spanish in the word ocho.

HISTORICAL LINGUISTICS: (Lingüística histórica). Sometimes called Philology in the United States, it is that branch of linguistics interested in the historical origin and development of language(s).

HYPERCORRECTION: (Ultra-corrección). A sometimes inaccurate form of a word used by native speakers in pursuit of a more prestigious manner of speaking. In Spanish such speakers might say*Bilbado instead of Bilbao, or use [v] instead of [b] and [ƀ] in Viven en Madrid.

IDIOLECT: (Idiolecto). The unique manner in which an individual speaks a language.

Idioma or Lengua: Language.

INCHOATIVE SUFFIX: (Sufijo incoativo). Sometimes called an inceptive suffix as well, it expresses the initial stage of the state or action conveyed by the stem. For example, an inchoative suffix, -ecer in enriquecer, changes the adjective "rich" to the verb "to enrich, to become rich." (Chapter 3).

Incrustamiento: Embedding.

INDEPENDENT or FREE MORPHEME: (Morfema independiente). A morpheme which is meaningful when articulated in isolation, such as en, por, hombre, mujer.

INDO-EUROPEAN: (Indoeuropeo). The very large and important family of languages to which belong most of the languages of Europe and India. The Germanic languages and the Romance languages are members of the Indo-European Family of languages.

INFIX: (Infijo). A type of affix, rare in English and Spanish which is added inside the stem or base. Some linguists suggest that -ar- is an infix in the word polvareda. (Chapter 3).

INFLECTION: (Inflexión). A morphological change in a stem or base created by the addition of an affix which does not change the form class or the basic meaning of the stem. Verb conjugations in Spanish are examples of inflection, as in amo, amas, ama, etc.

Intensión: On-glide.

INTONATION: (Entonación). The meaningful musicality of a language, including pitch and stress. (Chapter 2).

ISOGLOSS: (Isoglosa). A line drawn on a map by a dialect geographer, dividing one dialectical usage (or language) from another.

KINEGRAPHS: A system of noting facial expression.

KINESICS: The study of gestures used on comminication.

Lámina: Blade.

LANGUAGE: (Idioma or lengua). A system of sounds

used to convey meaning when presented orally or in writing within the acceptable limits of a language structure. (Introduction).

LANGUAGE FAMILY: (Familia de lenguas). A group of languages (like the Romance languages) which are related to each other because of having the same ancestor (as Latin, for example). (Introduction).

LATERAL: (Lateral). A consonant which is produced by allowing the air stream to pass on both sides of the tongue. An example is the /l/ in fila. (Chapter 2).

Latín clásico: Classical Latin.

Latín vulgar: Vulgar Latin.

LEARNED FORM: (Forma culta). Also called a cultismo in Spanish, it denotes a word of classical origin (usually Latin or Greek) which has not undergone the sound changes normal to other words of the same origin. Two examples in Spanish are fructífero and artículo. (Chapter 5).

Lengua: Tongue; Language.

Léxico: Lexicon.

LEXICOGRAPHY: (Lexicografía). The writing or compilation of a dictionary.

LEXICON: (Léxico). The stock of words belonging to a language. Sometimes it is used to denote a specialized set of terms used in a particular profession or subject.

LINGUISTICS: (Lingüística). The scientific study of language.

MANNER OF ARTICULATION: (Modo de articulación). The manner in which a sound is made, whether it be a stop, a fricative, an affricate, a lateral, a nasal, a tap, or a trill.

176

METAPHOR: (Metáfora). In semantics, the change in meaning due to a metaphorical association. In Spanish an example is the use of the word hoja when referring to a sheet of paper. (Chapter 6).

METATHESIS: (Metátesis). The transposition of letters within a word. It may be simple, as in SIBILARE>silbar, or reciprocal as in ANIMALIA>alimaña. (Chapter 5).

MINIMAL PAIRS: (Cotejos). The means by which linguists are able to derive phonemic, morphemic and syntactic values. A pair of words or phrases are used to distinguish one single element, as in the examples, pito/ pino and mala/masa.

Modo de articulación: Manner of articulation.

MONOPHTHONGIZATION: (Monoptongación). The process whereby a diphthong is reduced to a single vowel, as in AURUM>oro, in which the diphthong au becomes the monophthong (vowel) o. (Chapter 5).

Morfema dependiente: Dependent or Bound morpheme.

Morfema independiente: Independent or Free morpheme.

MORPHEME: (Morfema). The smallest unit of meaning in a language. Spanish examples include mujer, -cita, and -s in mujercitas. (Chapter 3).

MORPHOLOGY: (Morfología). The study of morphemes.

NARROWING or RESTRICTION OF MEANING: (Restricción del significado or Especialización). A historical semantic change in which the word being analyzed has a specialized, more narrow meaning than it had previously. As an example, SECARE in Latin meant "to cut," while in Spanish segar means "to harvest," a narrower, more specialized form of cutting. (Chapter 6).

NASAL: (Nasal). The class of consonants characterized by the passage of the air stream through
the nasal passage, as the /m/ and /n/ of
mina.

NASAL PASSAGE: (Cavidad nasal). The cavity behind
the nose used for respiration and for the production of nasal consonants or vowels.

Nivel de tono: Pitch.

NON-CONTIGUOUS ASSIMILATION: (Asimilación a distancia or Asimilación armónica). The historical process whereby two unlike sounds
(usually vowels) separated in a word by
intervening sounds become alike. The i e of
DIRECTU become e e in derecho. (Chapter 5).

NOUN: Sustantivo.

NOUN DETERMINER: (Determinante or Determinativo).
A term used to label those words which modify
a noun in a noun phrase (as part of transformational grammar), often a definite or
indefinite article such as la and una.

Oclusivo: Stop.

OFF-GLIDE: (Distensión). A term frequently
applied to the semivowel of a diphthong
because of its decreasingly vowel-like
nature. (Chapter 2).

ON-GLIDE: (Intensión). A term frequently applied
to the semiconsonant of a diphthong because
of its decreasingly consonant-like nature.
(Chapter 2).

ONOMASTICS: (Onomástica). A study of the names
of places, people and things. (Chapter 1).

Organos de articulación: Articulatory apparatus.

Organos de fonación: Voice box. (The vocal cords
and the larynx.)

178

Organos de respiración: Respiratory organs.

ORTHOGRAPHIC TRADITION: (Tradición ortográfica).
A term used to explain the traditional
spelling of words which have "silent"
letters, such as hombre and psicología—
in both cases the unpronounced initial letter
is an example of the orthographic tradition
in Spanish. Also part of this tradition is
the change of spelling required to preserve
the sound [k] in the historical development
CASEUM>queso. (Chapter 5).

Paladar: Hard palate.

PALATALIZATION: (Palatalización). The process
of creating a palatal sound where there was
none before. Usually it results from the
combining of two non-palatal consonants into
a single palatal, as in the example LIGNUM>
leño. The g [g] was velar, the n [n]
alveolar or alveodental, and the two became
simplified/combined into a single palatal
[ñ] through palatalization. (Chapter 5).

PARADIGM: (Paradigma). A list of all the inflectional forms of a word.

Parasíntesis: Simultaneous affixation.

PATRONYMICS: (Patronimia). The study of family
names.

PEJORATIVE: (Despectivo or Peyorative). As a
result of the process of pejoration, a word
comes to have a disparaging or downgraded
meaning. In Spanish a number of derivational
suffixes create pejoratives such as amigacho
and poetastro. As the result of worsening
semantic values, historically some words
have become pejoratives, such as chulo and
golfo.

PHILOLOGY: (Filología). In the United States,
philology is essentially equivalent to
historical linguistics, and is therefore the

179

study of the history and development of language. In Spanish the word filología denotes a meaning which includes literary studies as well, especially those dealing with the classics.

PHONEME: (Fonema). The minimum sound-unit of speech which distinguishes one word or utterance from another. The difference between words in the following set is phonemic: pito, piso, pino, pico, pido, as is also the difference between the two utterances, Es mi amigo, and ¿Es mi amigo?. (Chapter 2).

PHONETICS: (Fonética). The scientific study of the sounds of speech.

PHONOLOGICAL DETERMINATION or CONDITIONING: In discussing morphology, the allomorphs of a given morpheme are often said to be phonologically determined. For example, two major allomorphs of the morpheme plural, -s, added to most words ending in a vowel and to some foreign words, and -es, added to most words ending in a consonant, are said to be phonologically conditioned because their distribution is determined by the phonological environment. (Chapter 3).

PHONOLOGY: (Fonología). The scientific study of the sound system of language, including phonetics and phonemics (the study of phonemes).

PHRASE STRUCTURE RULES: (Reglas de estructura sintagmática). In transformational grammar the phrase structure rules are used to create the formal description of the grammatical structure of a sentence. (Chapter 4).

PITCH: (Nivel de tono). A part of intonation, it is the musical tone or sound-frequency of the voice used during the production of a meaningful utterance. The difference in Spanish between Estás aquí and ¿Estás aquí?

180

is one of pitch. (Chapter 2).

PLOSIVE: A term, like explosive which is sometimes
used in linguistics as the equivalent of the
term used in this book, STOP (oclusivo).
It is named for the sudden rush of air that
follows the release of many stops.

PLUS and MINUS FEATURES: The kind of feature nota-
tion favored by the transformationalists
whereby the elements of a language (sounds,
morphemes, words) are noted as having (indicated with a +) or not having (indicated
by a -) certain features. For example, the
/u/ is described in this system as plus (+)
vocalic, continuant, voice, high, back,
and minus (-) consonantal, nasal, low,
etc, (Chapter 2).

POINT or PLACE OF ARTICULATION: (Punto or Lugar
de articulación). The location in the mouth
where a (meaningful) sound is produced.
The point of articulation for the r of mira
is alveolar.

PREFIX: (Prefijo). An affix attached to the front
of a word.

PROGRESSIVE ASSIMILATION: (Asimilación progresiva).
It occurs when the first sound in a sound
cluster (group of sounds) influences the
second, as in PALUMBA>paloma, where the m
has influenced the b and has caused it to
disappear. (Chapter 5).

PROTHESIS: (Prótesis). The addition of a phoneme
at the beginning of a word. In Spanish, the
most common prothesis is the e- added
historically to words beginning with a
consonant cluster consisting of s followed
by a stop. Examples include: SPATHAM>espada,
and SCUTUM>escudo. (Chapter 5).

PROTO-: A prefix used to indicate the theoretical
reconstruction of the earliest stage of an
undocumented language or form.

PROVERB: (Refrán). A folk saying which expresses in a pithy manner a well-known truth or fact. It often has internal rhyme or uses assonance (vowel rhyme) to match the two parts of a parallel structure. Examples include: <u>No con quien naces sino con quien paces</u>, and <u>Poderoso caballero es don Dinero</u>.

Punto or Lugar de articulación: Point or Place of articulation.

Raíz: Stem, Root or Base (form).

Refrán: Proverb.

REGRESSIVE ASSIMILATION: (Asimilación regresiva). It occurs when the second sound in a sound cluster influences the first. In the word <u>mismo</u>, the phoneme /s/, pronounced [z] is voiced because of the voicing influence of the <u>m</u>. (Chapter 2).

RESPIRATORY ORGANS: (Organos de respiración). The lungs, the bronchi and the trachea.

RETROFLEX: (Retroflejo or cacuminal). A sound (usually a consonant) produced with the tip of the tongue flexed back toward the roof of the mouth. The American English /r/ in <u>roar</u> is a good example.

Reglas de estructura sintagmática: Phrase structure rules.

Restricción del significado: Narrowing or Restriction of meaning.

RISING DIPHTHONG: (Diptongo creciente). A diphthong consisting of a semiconsonant plus a vowel, as in the word <u>cien</u> [syen].

ROMANCE LANGUAGES: (Lenguas romances). The languages that developed from Vulgar Latin, including: Spanish, French, Italian, Portuguese, Rumanian, Catalan, Provençal, Rhaeto-Romance and Sardinian.

SEGMENTAL FEATURES: (Elementos segmentales). The sound system of a language excluding intonation, but including vowels, consonants, semiconsonants and semivowels.

SEMICONSONANT: (Semiconsonante). Sometimes called on-glide, the semiconsonant is the first half of a diphthong that ends in a vowel. The diphthong in <u>bien</u> [byen] contains a semiconsonant followed by a vowel.

SEMI-LEARNED FORM: (Forma semiculta). Also known as a semicultismo in Spanish, it describes a word which has undergone more historical sound changes than a cultismo, but not as many as a popular word. Two examples are SAECULUM>siglo and ECCLESIAM> iglesia. They are both semi-learned in that the <u>cl</u> cluster becomes <u>gl</u>. In a popular word, <u>cl</u> normally becomes <u>ch</u>, as in the development of TECULLUM>techo. (Chapter 5).

SESEO: The characteristic pronunciation of most of Spanish America in which the <u>c</u> of <u>c</u>inco and the <u>z</u> of <u>z</u>apato are pronounced as an [s].

SIMPLIFICATION: (Simplificación). A kind of complex assimilation in which two sounds combine to form one. An example of simplification is the change from <u>au</u> to <u>o</u> in PAUCUM>poco. (Chapter 5).

SIMULTANEOUS AFFIXATION: (Parasíntesis). In morphology, simultaneous affixation occurs when a prefix and a suffix are added at the same time, such as in creating the inchoative verbs, <u>engrandecer</u> and <u>empobrecer</u>. (Chapter 3).

Sinalefa: Synalepha.

Síncopa: Syncope.

Sintaxis: Syntax.

SLIT FRICATIVE: (Fricativa alargada). The class of fricatives characterized by the narrow horizontal slit created in their articulation. The f in sofá and the b in lobo are two examples in Spanish of slit fricatives.

Sonoridad: Voicing.

SONORIZATION: (Sonorización). The historical voicing of an unvoiced sound, as in CEPULLAM> cebolla, in which the p is voiced to b.

SPIRANT: (Espirante). A term sometimes used to name a class of consonant phonemes to which the /s/ and /h/ might belong.

STEM or BASE: (Raíz or Base). That part of a word to which derivational and inflectional affixes are added.

STOP: (Oclusivo). Also occasionally called an occlusive in English, as well as a plosive, it is a consonant phoneme characterized by the momentary stoppage of the air passage, as the p in mapa and the t in mata.

STRESS: (Acento de intensidad). The loudness of a syllable in an utterance. The difference between éste and esté is one of stress.

STRUCTURAL TREE: (Arbol estructural). The graphic representation of the relationship between the deep structure and the surface structure is shown by the transformationalists with a structural tree. (Chapter 4).

SUBSTRATUM: (Sustrato). The influence of a previous language upon the development of a later one, such as the influence of the Celtic or Iberian languages upon the development of Vulgar Latin into Spanish. (Chapter 1).

SUFFIX: (Sufijo). An affix added to the end of a stem, as for example -illo added to the stem, Juan, to form Juanillo.

Sufijo incoativo: Inchoative suffix.

SURFACE STRUCTURE: (Estructura superficial).
     The actual structure of a sentence, what is
     heard and/or seen.

Sustantivo: Noun.

SUPRASEGMENTAL FEATURES: (Elementos supraseg-
     mentales). The phonemic elements of intona-
     tion, including pitch, stress and glottal
     closure. (Chapter 2).

"SYLLABIC-r": In American English, a final
     unstressed syllable ending in r often contains
     what is known as the "syllabic-r". The
     final syllables of the following words exem-
     plify the phenomenon: tinkerer, butterer,
     wiper. American English also makes extensive
     use of the "syllabic-l" and the "syllabic-n."
     (Chapter 2).

SYNALEPHA: (Sinalefa). The linking of words in
     a sentence. The vowel on one word's end is
     joined to the initial vowel which follows,
     as in una artista [unartista].

SYNCOPE: (Síncopa). The loss of a sound or group
     of sounds from the middle of a word, such as
     the loss of the u in the development of
     INSULA>isla. (Chapter 5).

SYNTAX: (Sintaxis). The way in which words are
     put together to form phrases or sentences.

TAP or FLAP: (Vibrante simple). A consonant sound
     made when the tip of the tongue rapidly
     strikes the alveolar ridge, as if for a very
     short stop. An example is the /r/ of corta.

Tongue: Lengua.

TONIC ACCENT: (Acento de intensidad). Also
     called stress, it is the loudness of a
     syllable in an utterance.

TOPONYMY: (Toponimia). The study of place names.

TRANSFORMATIONAL GRAMMAR: (Gramática transformativa). Transformational grammar is a system of rules that generates sentences and which describes these sentences in a systematic manner.

Triángulo de vocales: Vowel triangle.

TRILL: (Vibrante múltiple). A rapid vibration or tapping of the tip of the tongue against the alveolar ridge, as the /r̄/ of hierro and perro. (Chapter 2).

TRIPHTHONG: (Triptongo). A compound vowel sound consisting of a semiconsonant, a vowel and a semivowel, as in the words, buey [bwei] and averguáis [aberigwais]. (Chapter 2).

Ultracorrección: Hypercorrection.

Variación libre: Free variation.

Vasco or Vascuence: Basque.

VELARIZATION: (Velarización). The process by which a sound is displaced in its point of articulation and moved towards the velum. The usual change is from palatal to velar, as in the development of OCULUM>oclo>*ollo> ojo, in which velarization describes the final step in its development. (Chapter 5).

VELUM: (Velo). The soft part of the roof of the mouth behind the hard palate, sometimes called the soft palate. The Spanish /k/ and /g/ are both velar sounds in the words kiosko, casa and inglés. (Chapter 2).

VIBRANT: (Vibrante). A term sometines used in English to identify both the tap or flap (vibrante simple) and the trill (vibrante múltiple).

Vibrante múltiple: Trill.

Vibrante simple: Tap or flap.

VOCAL CORDS: (Cuerdas vocales). Bands in the
larynx which vibrate when tightened and
which produce voiced sound as the air
stream passes.

Vocales: Vowels.

VOCALIZATION: (Vocalización). The (historical)
change from a consonant to a vowel, as in
the change from medieval cibdad to modern
ciudad. The b has become u through vocalization. (Chapter 5).

VOICE BOX: (la Laringe). The pharynx, called
the voice box popularly because it contains
the vocal cords.

VOICED "T": A term used in some speech texts to
name the voiced alveolar tap common in English in such words as water and butter, and
transcribed in this book as [r].

VOICING: (Sonoridad). The quality of a sound produced through vibration of the vocal cords.
Such a sound is said to be VOICED. When the
vocal cords do not vibrate the sound produced is said to be UNVOICED or VOICELESS.

VOWELS: (Vocales). Voiced sounds produced with
a shaping of the air stream but virtually
no obstruction of it. Consonants are shaped
by obstructing the air stream in some manner.

VOWEL TRIANGLE: (Triángulo de vocales). A graphic
means of showing approximate relationships and
positions of the vowels /i/ ＼ ／ /u/
in the mouth. The vowel /e/ ＼／ /o/
triangle for Spanish pho- /a/
nemes at the right is an illustration.

VULGAR LATIN: (Latín vulgar). The common, spoken
Latin of ancient Rome which developed into
the Romance languages (including Spanish).
It is distinct from Classical Latin which

187

was the language of literature.

Yeísmo: The tendency in much of the Spanish-speaking world of pronouncing the <u>ll</u> of <u>caballo</u> as if it were a <u>y</u> [kabayo].

YOD: (Yod). A term used by philologists to name the sound of the letter <u>i</u> and to describe the effect of palatal sounds on the historical development of vowels. In LACTEM>leche, the vowel <u>a</u> becomes <u>e</u> because of the "hidden" yod in the <u>ct</u> [kt] consonant cluster. Because of the yod, the Latin suffix -ARIA becomes -<u>era</u> in Spanish (Chapter 5).

SELECTED BIBLIOGRAPHY

The following list of books has been consulted
in the assembly of this text and represents a broad
spectrum of approaches and areas of interest. All
may be consulted for pleasure and profit by those
who find any of the topics treated in this text
of interest. Only books have been listed here,
but important articles appear regularly in many
of the professional journals.

Akmajian, Adrian, Richard A. Demers, & Robert M.
    Harnish. Linguistics: An Introduction to
    Language and Communication. Cambridge, Mass:
    MIT, 1979.
Alarcos Llorach, Emilio. Fonología española.
    Madrid: Gredos, 1965.
Alonso, Amado. De la pronunciación medieval a la
    moderna en español. 2 vols. Madrid: Gredos,
    1967-69.
Alonso, Amado. Estudios lingüísticos: Temas es-
    pañoles. Rpt. Madrid: Gredos, 1967.
Alonso, Amado. Estudios lingüísticos: Temas his-
    panoamericanos. Rpt. Madrid: Gredos, 1967.
Alvarez Nazario, Manuel. El influjo indígena en
    el español de Puerto Rico. Rio Piedras, PR:
    UPRED, 1977.
Arlotto, Anthony. Introduction to Historical
    Linguistics. Boston: Houghton Mifflin, 1972.
Beinhauer, Werner. El español coloquial. Tr.
    Fernando Huarte Morton. Rpt. Madrid: Gredos,
    1968.
Beinhauer, Werner. El humorismo en el español
    hablado. Madrid: Gredos, 1973.
Bloomfield, Leonard. Language. 1933 rpt. New
    York: Holt, Rinehart & Winston, 1961.
Bowen, J. Donald, & Jacob Ornstein, eds. Studies
    in Southwest Spanish. Rowley, Mass: Newbury
    House, 1976.
Bowen, J. Donald, & Robert P. Stockwell. Patterns
    of Spanish Pronunciation: A Drillbook.
    Chicago: U. of Chicago P., 1960.
Bull, William E. Spanish for Teachers: Applied
    Linguistics. New York: Ronald, 1965.
Canellada, María Josefa. Antología de textos
    fonéticos. Madrid: Gredos, 1965.

Canfield, D. Lincoln, & J. Cary Davis. An Intro-
    duction to Romance Linguistics. Carbondale:
    Southern Illinois UP, 1975.
Cárdenas, Daniel N. Introducción a una comparación
    fonológica del español y del inglés. Washing-
    ton, D.C.: Center for Applied Linguistics, 1960.
Corominas, Joan. Breve diccionario etimológico de
    la lengua castellana. Madrid: Gredos, 1967.
Corominas, Joan. Diccionario crítico etimológico
    de la lengua española. 4 vols. Madrid: Gredos.
Dalbor, John B. Spanish Pronunciation: Theory and
    Practice. New York: Holt, Rinehart & Winston,
    1969.
Elcock, W. D. The Romance Languages. London: Faber
    & Faber, 1960.
Entwistle, W. J. The Spanish Language Together
    with Portuguese, Catalan and Basque. 1936
    rpt. London: Faber & Faber, 1969.
Fente Gómez, Rafael, Jesús Fernández Alvarez,
    & Lope G. Feijóo. El subjuntivo. Madrid:
    SGEL, 1972.
Gili Gaya, Samuel. Elementos de fonética general.
    Rpt. Madrid: Gredos, 1966.
Gili Gaya, Samuel. Nociones de gramática histórica
    española. Rpt. Barcelona: Bibliograf, 1966.
Gleason, H. A., Jr. An Introduction to Descriptive
    Linguistics. New York: Holt, Rinehart &
    Winston, 1961.
Grandgent, C. H. An Introduction to Vulgar Latin.
    1934 rpt. New York: Hafner, 1962.
Green, Jerald R. A Gesture Inventory for the Teach-
    ing of Spanish. Philadelphia: Chilton, 1968.
Green, Jerald R. Spanish Phonology for Teachers:
    A Programmed Introduction. Philadelphia:
    Center for Curriculum Development, 1970.
Hadlich, Roger L. Gramática transformativa del
    español. Tr. Julio Bombín. Madrid: Gredos,
    1973.
Harris, James. Spanish Phonology. Cambridge,
    Mass: MIT, 1969.
Iribarren, José María. El porqué de los dichos.
    Rpt. Madrid: Aguilar, 1974.
Jeffers, Robert J., & Ilse Lehiste. Principles and
    Methods for Historical Linguistics. Cambridge,
    Mass: MIT, 1979.

Jespersen, Otto. Language: Its Nature, Development
    and Origin. Rpt. New York: W. W. Norton, 1964.
Kadler, Eric H. Linguistics and Teaching Foreign
    Languages. New York: Van Nostrand, 1970.
Kany, Charles E. American-Spanish Euphemisms.
    Berkeley: U. of California P., 1960.
Kany, Charles E. American-Spanish Semantics.
    Berkeley: U. of California P., 1960.
Kany, Charles E. American-Spanish Syntax. 1951
    rpt. Chicago: U. of Chicago P., 1967.
Lapesa, Rafael, ed. Comunicación y lenguaje.
    Madrid: Karpos, 1977.
Lapesa, Rafael, Historia de la lengua española.
    Rpt. Madrid: Escelicer, 1959.
Lausberg, Heinrich. Lingüística románica. 2 vols.
    Madrid: Gredos, 1966.
Lázaro Carreter, Fernando. Diccionario de términos
    filológicos. Rpt. Madrid: Gredos, 1971.
López Morales, Humberto, ed. Corrientes actuales
    en la dialectología del caribe hispánico.
    Río Piedras. PR: UPRED, 1978.
Mackey, Ian. Introducing Practical Phonetics.
    Boston: Little, Brown, 1978.
Maldonado, Felipe C. R., ed. Refranero clásico
    español y otros dichos populares. Madrid:
Menéndez Pidal, Ramón. Manual de gramática
    Histórica española. Rpt. Madrid: Espasa-
    Calpe, 1968.
Narváez, Ricardo A. An Outline of Spanish Morpho-
    logy. St. Paul, MN: EMC, 1970.
Narváez, Ricardo A. Instruction in Spanish
    Pronunciation. 2 vols. St. Paul: EMC, 1969-70.
Navarro Tomás, Tomás. Estudios de fonología
    española. 1946 rpt. New York: Hafner, 1961.
Navarro Tomás, Tomás. Manual de pronunciación
    española. 1957 rpt. New York: Hafner, 1961.
Pequeño Larousse ilustrado. Paris: Larousse, 1967.
Politzer, Robert L., & Charles N. Staubach.
    Teaching Spanish: A Linguistic Orientation.
    Lexington, Mass: Xerox, 1965.
Posner, Rebecca. The Romance Languages. Garden
    City: Doubleday Anchor, 1966.
Ramsey, Marathon Montrose. A Textbook of Modern
    Spanish. Revised by Robert K. Spaulding.
    New York: Holt, Rinehart & Winston, 1965.

191

Recio Flores, Sergio. Diccionario comparado de
    refranes y modismos, español-inglés. Sal-
    tillo, Mexico: 1968.
Real Academia Española. Esbozo de una nueva
    gramática de la lengua española. Madrid:
    Espasa-Calpe, 1973.
Rodríguez Adrados, Francisco. Lingüística estruc-
    tural. 2 vols. Madrid: Gredos, 1969.
Smith, Colin, with Manuel Bermejo Marcos, &
    Eugenio Chang-Rodriguez. Collins Spanish-
    English, English-Spanish Dictionary.
    London: Collins, 1971.
Spaulding, Robert K. How Spanish Grew. 1945 rpt.
    Berkeley: U. of California P., 1965.
Stockwell, Robert P., J Donald Bowen, & John W.
    Martin. The Grammatical Structures of
    English and Spanish. Chicago: U. of Chicago
    P., 1965.
Stockwell, Robert P., & J. Donald Bowen. The
    Sounds of English and Spanish. Chicago:
    U. of Chicago P., 1965.
Terrell, Tracy D., & Maruxa Salgués de Cargill.
    Lingüística aplicada a la enseñanza del español
    a angloparlantes. New York: John Wiley, 1979.
Traupman, John C. The New Collegiate Latin &
    English Dictionary. New York:Bantam, 1966.
Von Wartburg, Walther. La fragmentación lingüís-
    tica de la Romania. Tr. Manuel Muñoz Cortés.
    Rpt. Madrid: Gredos, 1971.
Wardhaugh, Ronald. Introduction to Linguistics.
    New York: McGraw-Hill, 1972.
Williams, Edwin B. The Williams Spanish & English
    Dictionary. 1963 rpt. New York: Charles
    Scribner's, 1972.
Zamora Vicente, Alonso. Dialectología española. Rpt.
    Madrid: Gredos, 1970.

INDEX

Affix, 89, 90, 91, 95, 96, 97, 105, 165, 175, 181, 184

   Infix, 89, 91, 165, 175

   Prefix, 21, 89, 104-105, 165, 181, 183

   Suffix, 10, 19, 20, 89, 91-94, 98-103, 140, 183, 184

Affixation, 89-90, 165

Affricate, 37, 50, 51, 52, 53-54, 66, 165, 176

Alfonso X, El Sabio, 23-24

Allomorph, 85-90, 109, 165

Allophone, 12, 34, 38-76, 85

Altaic, 5

Alveolar (Ridge), 35, 36, 41, 42, 45, 48, 54, 55, 56, 62, 103, 187

Ameliorative, 146-47, 148, 166

Analogy, 40, 121-22, 124, 128, 166

Apex, 36, 166

Apheresis, 122, 128, 166

Apocope, 122, 128, 130, 138, 140, 166

Appendix _Probi_, 132

Applied Linguistics, 166

Appreciative, 102, 103, 166

Arab(s)/Arabic, 5, 17, 18, 19-22, 149, 174

Araucan Indians, 25

Arawak: See Caribbean Indians

Articulatory Apparatus, 35, 36-37, 167

Aspiration, 12, 39, 43-44, 45, 167

Assimilation, 122, 129, 167, 183

   Progressive, 122-23, 129, 167, 181

   Regressive, 49, 59, 72, 122-23, 129, 167, 182

   Non-Contiguous, 123, 129, 167, 178

Augmentative, 91, 102, 103, 167

Base/Stem, 5, 90, 105, 168, 184, 189

Hannibal, 14

Haplology, 128, 130, 174

Hapsburgs, 8, 27

Hard Palate/Palatal, 35,
36, 48, 49, 50, 54,
55, 56, 58, 59, 62,
126, 136, 167, 174,
186

Historical Linguistics,
6, 121, 174

Huns, 17

Hypercorrection, 40, 174

Iberian(s), 9-10, 12,
168, 184

Idiolect, 8, 174

Inchoative Suffix, 90,
101, 174-75, 183

Independent/Free Morpheme:
See Morpheme

Indo-European, 3, 4, 175

Infix: See Affix

Inflection, 90, 91-94,
95, 96, 175

Intensifier, 105

Internal Reconstruc-
tion, 4

Intonation, 33, 76-82,
175, 180, 185

Isogloss, 7, 175

Italian Influence, 26

Jones, Sir William, 3

Julián, Conde, 19-20

Kemke, Andreas, 3

Kinegraphs, 175

Kinesics, 2, 175

Language Family, 3-6, 176

Language Isolate, 5

Lateral, 52, 54-56, 66-
67, 176

Learned Form, 125, 129,
176

Lexicography, 176

Lexicon, 9, 10, 11, 16,
18-19, 21-22, 23, 24-
25, 26, 28, 29, 30,
145, 176

Ligurii, 9

Linguistics, Definition,
1, 176

Manner of Articulation,
37, 38-76, 176

Mayan, 1, 5, 25

Menéndez Pidal, Ramón,
138, 144, 191

Metaphor, 147, 148, 177

Metathesis, 125, 129, 141,
177

Plosive, 38, 181, 184

Plus and Minus Features, 37, 74-76, 115, 171, 181

Point/Place of Articulation, 37, 38-76, 181

Portuguese(-Galician), 6, 18, 24

Prefix: See Affix

Preterit/Imperfect, 154-57

Progressive Assimilation: See Assimilation

Prothesis, 126, 129, 181

Proto-, 4, 181

Proverb, 72-73, 182

Punic Wars, 13

Qualitative/Quantitative Language, 16, 139, 140-41, 168

Quechua, 6, 25

Regressive Assimilation: See Assimilation

Relative Clause Maker, 119

Retroflex, 59-61, 182

Rodrigo, 19-20

Romance Languages, 6, 140, 175, 176, 182

Sanskrit, 3

Schwa, 69

Segmental Phonemes/ Features, 33, 37, 38-76, 77, 183

Semantics, 1, 145-50, 171, 177

Semiconsonant, 34, 35, 50, 51, 52, 53, 70, 135, 183, 186

Semi-Learned Form, 125, 129, 183

Semivowel, 34, 52, 71, 135, 183, 186

Ser/Estar, 151-54

Seseo, 25-26, 183

Simplification, 126, 127, 130, 135, 138, 139, 183

Simultaneous Affixation, 89-90, 100, 183

Sonorization, 12, 124, 130, 139, 141, 184

Spirant, 51, 184

Stem: See Base

Stop, 12, 37, 38-46, 53, 66, 128, 167, 176, 184

Unreleased Stop, 39

Stress, 70, 76, 79-81, 97, 133, 165, 175, 184, 185